Medicine Woman Speaks ™

Experienced, Written,
and Created by:

Lizette Rodriguez

Life is Beautiful

There are no words to describe
The randomness of everything
The perfection of everything
The chaos of everything

. . . all in one neat little bubble of life.

2014, Lexington

My Prayer

Through this book,
may a spark of the flame
ignited in me
pass onto you.

Life Is Beautiful

ISBN: 978-0-9916135-0-2
Library of Congress Control Number: 2014908582

Publisher's Cataloging-in-Publication - *Provided by Quality Books, Inc.*

Rodriguez, Lizette.
    Life is Beautiful / Experienced, written, and created
    by Lizette Rodriguez.
      pages cm
    Includes bibliographical references.
      LCCN 2014908582
      ISBN 978-0-9916135-0-2

    1. Rodriguez, Lizette. 2. Women shamans--Biography.
    I. Title.
BP610.R63A3 2014   299.8
               QBI14-600190

Flower/Vitruvian Man logo (TM) design by: Sandra Castro - SYC Media
Editorial Support: Sandy Suminski
Feather Design: Iona Mize

For more information regarding quantity discounts for educational purposes, fundraising, training, special events, reading groups, premiums, and sale promotions, please contact us at: *book@MedicineWomanSpeaks.com.*

Disclaimer: Someday in the near future, there will be no need to speak these words – but in the meantime – use your personal power and responsibility to gain the experience of accountability with how you work on and employ the material found in this book. Work this material with proper order based on your current capabilities and abilities. The material here in no way negates or is a substitute for medical and mental health treatment or advice. This, in itself, is a lesson. Everything has its place and purpose – including medical treatment.

Published by

Medicine Woman Speaks, LLC
P.O. Box 2106
Lexington, KY 40588

book@MedicineWomanSpeaks.com

To the Spirits of whom we are.
To the past that lights our path.
To the present that shows us the way,
And to the future that leads us onward.

Dedication

---•✧•---

This book is dedicated to the child who opened the floodgates; who pushed me endlessly and restlessly; who gambled with the rushing waters along my side; who treaded and navigated so earnestly; who alongside me – pointed out the light, the path, when needed; who expanded my growth beyond the reaches of my imagination.

May I have in some small way done the same.

Gracias hijita, mi Yadira*.

Gracias hijita, mi Yadira: Spanish for "Thank you, my dear daughter, Yadira."

CONTENTS

INTRODUCTION

CHAPTERS

an INVITATION

PROLOGUE

What can be more beautiful than taking the pain
of the heart, placing it between your hands,
and seizing the opportunity through the glory
of Love and Life to transform your pain into
the dove of peace and freedom for the soul?

We are not alone. Life is alive, the world is alive, and alive with every intention to assist and care for us, and more, to help us open our eyes to the moment's beauteous workings of Life[1] itself. The world wants us to learn, to grow and become educated in the fine wisdom, knowledge, and teachings of the sacred, the religious and the spiritual, of all that we as individuals encompass, and that as a whole we compose. The world also wants us to fall into the idea of having the consciousness of living a life, within Life itself.

Life entices us to observe, recognize and witness that She is beautiful no matter the experience lived. She calls out to us to honor and trust the totality of the experience that has entered our space. She allures each of us to be at a level of awareness and consciousness where we understand there is perfection in the moment, even if in those very moments we are unable to perceive the way in which those dots of experience connect to this perfection. She persuades us to be aware, if only for a glimpse, of the miracles that exist and occur in between the inhale and exhale of every breath of each moment.

Yet, Life does not want us to be still among the pain or injustice. On the contrary, a door opens so that we may reach for a total transformation and She presents the opportunity, particularly in the direst of situations, to seek, search, and find

---

[1] Lower case *"life:"* general meaning—it starts when we are born and ends when we die. Upper case *"Life:"* all our trajectory of birth, death, and rebirth—encompasses all of Life including and beyond our material and unseen worlds, dimensions, and spheres.

our Selves. Life insists we be a catalyst and an example, not only for our Selves, but also for others and for the world itself. So She pushes us to rise above the burdens of our cross, to make our path – our way – the catalyst for change, while we become an example to others of the internal transformation possible in each of us. Through this personal transformation, and with determination, we can go forth and bear fruit from our internal struggles, and provide nourishment to others. This may be through the simplest and smallest of kind gestures, or with giant leaps such as breaking personal or social barriers of repeated, automatic, and outdated actions created in response to life's tense structures and pain.

Life also wants to see us climb the ladder of knowledge and expand the height, width, and depth of our emotional intelligence, physical genius, spiritual insight, life wisdom and prudence.

Most of all, Life wants us to be happy, not only of the heart, but of the mind, of the soul, and of the spirit! And She wants us to recall and remember that no matter the steps taken, we are loved!

Indeed, a Beautiful Life – this package to behold!

INTRODUCTION

My Journey as a Medicine Woman

My journey and travels into becoming the instrument of the work I do today, that of a Medicine Woman using Spider[1] and Snake[2] Medicine, was truly an expedition beyond fantasy.

On one level, the process was in action long before I was born, and before I entered this segment of birth/death. On another level, I was born with clairvoyance, clairaudience, and strong extra-sensory perception abilities that allow me to directly feel and sense the emotional and physical bodies of others – in particular their discomfort and pain. Interesting, unusual experiences started when I was young, yet on a sporadic level as far as I recall. For instance, I could see skeletons when people passed on. Interesting concept at age five, but by nine years old it was getting pretty scary.

On another level, my official entry into the womanhood of Medicine Woman began in 2007. Over the years, there were a variety of catalysts that led to this significant moment. First, through the guidance of dreams, I met Dr. Arturo Estrada, a medical and metaphysical doctor, in my hometown of Bogota, Colombia in 1995. At that time, I was experiencing my first encounter with death. I was about to expire from my physical body, when, through his metaphysical insights, abilities, and capabilities, Dr. Estrada yanked me back to full capacity within my physical body. Since then, he has been my teacher of esoteric, metaphysical and spiritual studies. This experience merits a book of its own. Perhaps in the near future I will retell the surreal, intricate, and fascinating events of this near-death encounter and dance.

The second catalyst was the unknown implications of working with computers, and the effects they were having on

---

[1] **Spider Medicine**: Metaphysical, Mystical, and Spiritual medicine based on the knowledge of Spider energy. It is a horizontal female axis energy and its main purpose is creator.

[2] **Snake Medicine**: Metaphysical, Mystical, and Spiritual medicine based on the knowledge of Snake energy. It is a vertical female axis energy and its main purpose is communicator.

my etheric and physical body. This brought about a weakness and disturbance to my etheric body and eventually its collapse. The third catalyst was the passing of my mother in 1998. Her physical passing brought me to a space and time of a higher level of emotional and mental vibration. In addition, she works with healing on many capacities from where she is now, and my work is connected to her work.

Topping off the list of transforming catalysts was the entry into my life of my seven-year-old daughter – first through the Foster Care system, then through adoption. A child can be an enormous opportunity to converge upon one's self and discover what one is all about. All spotlights pointed on me, and the imminent heat was of the perfect temperature to begin the transformation I was to embark upon. And so I commenced my travels into the Dark Night of the Soul[1] in the winter of 2006.

A few years later, I picked up Caroline Myss' book *Sacred Contracts* and found the blueprint for the archetypal pattern I embodied on my walk through the Dark Night of the Soul. As I read Caroline's *Wounded Healer* archetype, I realized that this was what my Soul – the true me – had chosen as the story my Being would act out in this play of life. Along the way, when occasionally allowed, I took the reigns and directed my own creative endeavors.

Wounded Healer – Caroline's Description

"The wounded Healer is initiated into the art of healing through some form of personal hardship – anything from an actual physical injury or illness to the loss of all one's earthly possessions Regardless of the shape of the wound, the challenge inherent in this initiation process is that one is unable to turn to others for help beyond a certain degree of support. Only the initiate can ultimately heal the wound; if it is an illness or accident, it will frequently be one for which there is no conventional cure. The Wounded Healer archetype emerges in your psyche with the demand that you push yourself to a level of inner effort that becomes more a process of transformation than an attempt to heal an illness. If you have successfully completed the initiation, you inevitably experience an exceptional healing, and a path of service

---

[1] **Dark Night of the Soul**: Christian theology describes this as a period of spiritual desolation suffered by a mystic in which all sense of consolation is removed. (Oxford Dictionary).

seems to be divinely provided shortly after the Initiation process is complete."

Word for word, I followed this archetype. The injury, the solitary walk in the desert, the ineffectiveness and impossibility of conventional and unconventional healing methods, and then the exceptional healing. The process was a total transformation for me. I was able to pierce the shell of my Being and emerge and connect to my Higher Self, which then brought the connection to Spider Woman, who brought Her Knowledge and healing. Through Her force I healed myself physically, and up to this day I employ Her teachings in the healing work that I offer. The arduous Hero's journey I traveled has certainly provided a divine path of service to myself and to others.

"The Navajo have their own version of Spider Woman. As with all metaphors, Spider Woman is a bridge that allows a certain kind of knowledge to be transmitted from the mundane to the sacred dimension... They believe that an individual must undergo an initiation before he or she can be fully receptive to this kind of knowledge. Thus, to the eyes of the uninitiated, Spider Woman appears merely as an insect, and her words go unheard. But to the initiated whose mind has been opened, the voice of this tiny creature can be heard. This is the nature of the wisdom conveyed through the medicine of Spider Woman."

Cultural anthropologist Carol Patterson - Rudolph

The Struggle

The way of the Cross is not easy,
yet it is tuneful, the rhythmic,
the beautiful, the lovely way.

-Edgar Cayce
Reading 1089-6

*Everything and everyone struggles to live... the struggle is
beautiful... and, yes... it is real, too!*

In 2006, a particular set of incidents led to an injury and collapse of my etheric body's[1] structure. The struggle that slowly arose and ensued with full force, intensity and fierceness, was at a level of vigor previously unbeknownst to me. My etheric body breakdown rippled through my physical body, eventually causing an intense shift as every cell was abruptly and totally awakened by the onslaught of nerve pain.

Every imaginable door to Life flung open, and I became alive like never before to emotions, thoughts, feelings, and sensations as the pain radiated through every point of my flesh. In particular, the nerve pain ran across my shoulders, down my arms, hands, and up and down alongside my spinal column. The pain was unfailing, battering me 24 hours a day, every day for about six months. Eventually, I could not even open the refrigerator door, and most of my upper body mobility came to a halt. First, my arms started to stiffen, over time becoming locked in a manner similar to a first position ballet pose. My neck followed with stiffness, inflexibility and immobility. I could barely lie down for more than ten minutes, sleep was next to impossible, and sitting was an option for only about ten minutes at a time. No matter whom I sought for help there was

---

[1] *etheric body*: Less dense, subtle vehicle that is integrated into our physical body and provides the transporation of various energies including vitality to our physical body. It also functions on its own without the physical body.

4

no major relief. Living the moment took on a whole new meaning – all I could do was continuously pace back and forth down the memorable 50-foot-long hallway of my condo, persistently pierced by this surreal pain and discomfort.

I could not move physically or cosmically in any direction; forward, backward, diagonal, sideways, and L-shaped roads were blocked. With perfect moves – in this game of life – Life had me in checkmate! I was sentenced and confined to the cell of my Being, unable to run away or hide from myself. My mind and emotions were perfectly imprisoned within me, forcing me to firmly face, greet, and get to know who I am. Surrounded by my emotional walls and confined to my mind, I was graciously welcomed to roam and encounter this space within me. In the course of time, through this intimate engagement, I came to realize I was not my body, my emotions, nor my personality. I at last consciously encountered the separateness of my thoughts and brain activity from the Higher mind.

The emotional waves of this imprisonment savaged every crevice, corner, and innermost recess of my Being. I experienced mental anguish, alienation, desolation and abandonment. I felt misunderstood, dejected, and disheartened by the minimal support and reaching out of others. The pounding and onslaught in full attire by the fear and anger I felt on so many occasions was more than I could bear. I died a slow death. I would have let go and continued my journey into the next realm, but at the time, the carrot that dangled in front of me was the unbearable notion of adding another family loss to the life experience of my precious eight-year-old daughter Yadira. This was incentive enough for me to make the conscious decision to carry on living within this realm.

Literally and metaphysically, during a six-month period I walked between two worlds. The mind tried to hold its sanity and my soul cried out in torment in response to the rawness and fire lit within my body, my mind, and my emotions.

This continuous turmoil and attack on all fronts led me, on one fine day, to once again fall to my knees. As I had done so many times previously, I implored the gods to listen – in mercy, in anger, in resolution, in submission, in resignation, with ardent prayer, with total acceptance and peace. I let every word, thought, and emotion scatter out of me. It was, for me, another attempt in my plea to Life – to help me – to answer my questions of "Why? – Why me? – What have I done?" I was the whole range of emotions – blessing my imploration with an ample supply of tears that had touched the molten depths of earth's recorded pain and despair. Once again, when this episode ended, I felt that a clearing had occurred. I felt a moment's peace and a sense of relief.

On this particular day, I proceeded to the kitchen and sat on the wooden chair, feeling, if only for a few seconds, whole again. I was in thought about how, just days before, for the second time in this life frame of mine, I was less than a hair away from leaving this physical body. As I tell you this story, I recall, with a Mona Lisa smile, what happened next... and that was the moment when I felt the distinct placement of someone's hands on the back of my head, and the hands began to move my head. No one was home at this time and I wondered if it was my mom's hands that were moving my head. She had passed on in 1998.

The hands pressed on, trying to stretch and move my head side-to-side and front-to-back. I grunted and shrieked from the profound muscle and nerve pain experienced by a neck unaccustomed to such movement for over six months – yet I knew all was well with this moment, this event, this experience. I was at peace. I had surrendered, accepted, and submitted to what force was now part of me – and I part of it!

At one point I could no longer feel the hands, yet my head continued to move on its own, instinctively and knowingly. This movement then spread to my arms and hands, and eventually throughout my entire body, continuing for three days nonstop. Unbeknownst to me at that time, my Kundalini[1] had awakened; I was resurrecting, being born again; my physical body had recalled its primal wisdom and had entered a new realm of intelligence. My body and I were headed to new worlds and new heights.

This was only the start to the next chapter in this long, long astounding journey. What ensued was an intense metaphysical and esoteric initiation, and about six years of deep Life and self-discovery. I walked this journey assaulted by new levels of fear and anger, as if what I had experienced before was

---

[1] **Kundalini**: The spiritual mother/female primal force of the serpent energy that, in the human body, arises from the base of the spinal column and ascends upward in movement and expansion of knowledge.

not enough for several lifetimes. You may think most moments were joyous and happy for me – but at that time I was unaware and still too young of the mind – enough to not know, nor quite capture the special circumstance, the extraordinary, unique, and momentous distinction of this pilgrimage, and much less was I to know of Earth's current insistence that we find resolution among her lesson plans on duality[1]. Thus I continued to travel in emotional distraught, mental distress and anxiety, and insurmountable physical exhaustion.

I can now say, that eventually I saw the beauty beyond the curtain, the fog, and the darkness. I was able to incorporate the struggles and pain and comprehend they were needed in order to bring a balance to my Higher Self, and even more, that every action taken by others was truly in perfect sync, designed with precision so I could focus and evolve within and complete this particular Life expedition. This allowed me to form a bond of trust within myself, and consequently, I was able to establish a sincere and trusting relationship with the assistance and guidance offered by all who watch and care for us from other spheres and dimensions of Life. Through this mental balance and new outlook, I could then delight in the various opportunities and adventures lived on this fantastic, mystical path. Subsequently, I graciously accepted the gifts bestowed upon me for the effort and achievements in my *Life Studies*. In return, they have become my gifts to Life!

I felt like a mother who had just given birth – the joy, the overwhelming emotions of the miracle, the beauty of life and the newborn child overshadowed the labor pains, fear, and difficulties, and I could see the authentic beauty of all the marvels and jewels of my journey.

There is much beauty and wonder in all that is possible. There are New Lands to discover and explore, and so much more that exists beyond our narrowly forged walls and our cage of set beliefs. I share with you insights into some of the treasures that can be had, which I experienced within the layers and abundance of landscapes in this beautiful, astonishing, breathtaking and amazing Life: miraculous healings; entry into

---

[1] **duality**: Planet Earth is alive. She has emotions, thoughts, internal and external functions, and a purpose. She is going through a stage of fast growth and she pushes us to finish our third grade life studies. Part of her curriculum entails that we resolve duality. The three tiers being good/bad – Life/death – God/evil.

the underworld; visits with Quetzalcoatl, Egyptian Initiates, Queen Hatshepsut, Spider Woman, White Buffalo, an Angel of Death, and incredible encounters with the one called The Master, the one I call my brother, Jesus; being nurtured, cradled, and cared for by the Native American Indians of the upper realm; my internal transformations into an eagle, a snake, a dinosaur, an angel; communication with distant lands in other parts of this universe and travel to worlds few have encountered; the use of the frontal lobes of my brain and, with and through my eyes, the unbelievable work done on the physical level. I was shown the universal, symbolic, and vibrating written language of our solar system and the Milky Way; I combined both male and female physical (internal) and psychological characteristics, thus granting me the experience of an androgynous[1] Being; I experienced the entry of the profound and complete realm of love into my heart's space – allowing me to encounter the definite and absolute force of the true love that permeates from the soul; I experienced reality that could not even measure up to fantasy, and I touched a part of the incomprehensible world of who we are.

These are indeed precious jewels and memorable experiences. If it were not for the pain, turmoil, and despair, the essence of the flower would still be asleep within the seed that I am.

<blockquote>
Ahhh…the beautiful struggle!
I would have not known of the beauty
had it not been for the bloom.
</blockquote>

---

[1] **androgynous**: Having both male and female psychological and physical characteristics.

8

The Beautiful is the totality of the experience –
found within the separateness, the chaos,
and the Oneness that we are –
balanced and aligned with the awareness,
trust, and acceptance of the opportunities
and gifts the path that we walk brings us.

The Book

Life Is Beautiful is a compilation of various quotes, poems, aphorisms, snippets, revelations and statements that emerged as I lived my amazing journey and initiation. It is the product of moments of intense insight, awareness, experience and understanding as I traveled through a multitude of worlds within the layers of the holographic mind that we live in.

This mystical, metaphysical and esoteric journey was frightening, but nonetheless remarkable, awakening, adventurous, and full of discovery. I experienced in the flesh the Oneness of our Being; I touched incredible corners of my mind; I experienced emotions and my physical body in a way I would have never thought conceivable; I entered rooms of infinite Knowledge and rooms of never-ending Books; I inscribed in the Akashic Records[1]; sat at the negotiating table, reviewed and experienced past time, the present moment and future events. I saw that the likelihood of anything is probable and I intervened, fought for, entered and stood firm in the righteousness of my heart and the solidarity of my mind.

The result, after years of contemplating and writing about these magical events, the conversations held, and information captured within various realms of time and space, is this book. The purpose, for me, was to discover and enter into a new realm of "Who am I?" and "What am I?" May the purpose extend to the discovery of who you are, who we are, and to where this discovery will lead us.

---

[1] *Akashic Records*: A metaphysical library where books with all knowledge and every movement of time, light, and space are found. This includes the Life history of thoughts, words, energy, and action of each individual, the earth, our solar system, the Milky Way and beyond.

Dark Night of the Soul

*This is the season in which you are
prodded to answer the call of the Soul.*

If you are in times of darkness, in heaviness of the soul –
seek within and outside the self. You must continue to push
forward, to understand there is a reason and purpose for all you
have been, all that you are and will be. With all out effort,
intent, and determination, encourage yourself to persist through
the mud, snow, and rain as you work through your night. With
candor, visit and dissect every thought, fear, anger, and
emotion that races through the pages in your head and through
the waves of your emotional body. Getting to the core of your
beliefs is required; hope, faith, and determination will
consistently test you; disclose the agreements you have made to
your Lord and walk the fine Line of Fire[1] when needed. It helps
to remember the task at hand – individual and spiritual
freedom from the chains that bind us to our presumed
assumptions, which can be attained through the reconciliation
and resolution to the dualities of good/bad[2], Life/death, and
God/evil.

You too can pierce the shell, the lining – and connect
with your Higher Self, particularly at these times where the
forces are such that they provide the means to do so with ease.

Then, as you take flight and soar, no matter how high
you fly, how grand the upper realms open up to you or the
inner worlds or the underworld open up to you, always keep
grounded and centered, both in heart and mind. Keeping the
mind grounded means you have the awareness, capacity and
strength to continue working within the forces and the
boundaries of this earthly realm. It means you can acknowledge

---

[1] **Line of Fire**: An internal narrow path that opens between two walls of fire purifying
emotions. This is the same analogy as the parting of the Red Sea in Exodus – walking
the fine path between two walls of water.

[2] **good/bad**: This tier of duality encompasses other polarities such as: male/female,
light/dark, win/lose, yin/yang, negative/positive, etc.

when you need outside assistance and you know when to employ reason. Reason and the Mind stay in the equation when the other realms open up to you. After all, the Mind is the female aspect, the She energy of the body. Listen to Her with the reason and intelligence She brings and walk the tightrope between the two worlds that you encounter, with strength and balance.

So march forward in your discovery of who you are. A few scratches and bruises here and there are okay. Just get up, step forth, and continue to ride again.

As Edgar Cayce said...

Keep the Heart singing!
Keep the Mind clear!
Keep the face towards the light!
The shadows then fall behind.

Reading 39-4

The New World

The distinguishing factor between the "old world" and the New World is the change in light configuration. We have entered the New World and it has a higher vibrating light configuration than the "old world." The "end of the world" has already occurred, and the old light configuration no longer exists. The New World is also the world of the present in its newborn stage.

Fear not the new structure and the joy that is among us. The "End of the World" is the end of one light configuration, and the "New World" is the beginning of a new light configuration – the old light configuration no longer exists and the new light configuration is now in place. The light configuration gives the messages, codes, communication, instruction, and provides the mother seed vibration to all and everything. This is similar to the chemical signals produced within our body as a means of communication and instruction. You can say that this new light configuration is bringing humanity to a stage of adolescence, with all its trials, challenges, struggles, drama, and growth spurts. The change is inevitable, so hold on as humanity enters puberty and thus we commence our entry into a New World of higher understanding, elevated capabilities, abilities, and cognitive skills. At times, the mood pendulum will swing from one end to the other. Our work is to remain calm and centered during this whirlwind of change and development.

This process of adolescence and growth is sure to bring forth the needed capacity, structures, levels, entertainment, agreements and humor needed in any story telling; and the story of The New World will bring a sigh of relief, a relaxed fit and enjoyment, and moments of smiles, joy and laughter, all greatly needed and to be dispersed not amongst a select few, but among all Beings.

Furthermore, when we enter that highlighted moment and space of the New World where we become truly aware of these other walking bodies and living Beings around us – those we call family, friends, foes, pets, animals, flowers, trees and so forth – on that day we will truly, at heart and at depths of the mind, connect and recollect that we are them and they are us. Further still, when we can love beyond the pull, commitment and duty we feel within our bloodlines, and we can surpass this intimate circle of gravity and extend the same love, duty, and commitment outside of our inherited relationships – we will then have begun to truly live, to truly understand our mission and our purpose. Then we will be ready to begin our New World order of establishing His rightful Kingdom of Heaven here on Earth. This concept, understood within each of you personally in experience, outside of the simple understanding of my words, is what will enlighten anew the ring of fire within our hearts. Then the old laws will no longer apply. New realities will emerge, truths will shed their skin, the unthinkable and the unimaginable will become conceivable and our goal, achievable!

Hallelujah!

A Final Note

I bring you my interpretation of new levels of thought, ideas, and knowledge. Some information in this book is written verbatim as I received it. Some are my conclusions, understanding perceived, knowledge that opened up, or words of truth from the experience of the moment. Some writings are similar concepts or words written from a slightly different angle.

Accept not blindly, but upon presentation to your Selves and upon feedback from your inner guidance. Feel it. Question it. Discuss it, and see where and how it resonates in your world. Adjust this knowledge and level of truth to your acceptance, and incorporate those items that best fit and support the development of your present mental, emotional, physical, and spiritual light configuration.

If these words resonate with you – wonderful. Yet, keep in mind there is only so much my articulation can reach and touch within you – my words having little lasting effect compared to the experience in the flesh. I may speak of all things that are occurring and are possible, but until you can validate them with your mind, heart, and body in actual experience, can you then take the lessons learned as a guiding light for yourself and for others. This requires that you put the time and effort to become conscious of your thoughts, feelings, and emotions. Each one of us has our unique path, walk, and medicine. You must find yours.

My love and joy in everything
that you do and all that you are.

Medicine Woman Lizette

To all my lives –
May they unite as One.

———•●•———

For the children of God –
so they may step ahead and join the
ranks of wisdom, joy and love.

———•●•———

MY PIECE I GIVE YOU

Love

Be the utmost lover. Be in love with life.

— ·•· —

Joy and happiness are the flavoring
and seasoning to life.
Sprinkle them into your daily moments of life.

— ·•· —

You are a bright shining sun.
May you always shine forth and illuminate your
love, both in Heaven and on Earth.

— ·•· —

May all your successes
be in the realm of love, joy, and peace.

I WANT

I am inspired to no end
with the beauty within you.

I want to know what life has brought
and flowered upon your soul and
I want to hear what life has dipped
into your struggles, pain and grief.

I want to know about your dreams
and your hopes and
I want to feel the joy rides
and see the smiles and laughter you have had.

I want to caress the tenderness that you are and
I want to sit and take your hand
and know your heart.

I want to carefully see every move of your face
and feel every crease of your hand
and know of your travels
and simply stay
and feel the beauty
of all that you are.

PARTNERS IN THE DANCE OF LIFE

Become my partner in the dance of life.

How you ask?

Notice me. . . the Life that I am, your dance partner.
Notice me in your sweet inhale.
Notice me in your passionate exhale.
Together we meet in breath and dance.
Bring me in close to you.
Gently push me away but hold me tight
and bring me in again, and out.
In and out, in and out,
our breaths become the passionate breath of life.

———·•·——

Love has many vibrations

I have found my beloved!
He resides in me . . .
and I love him so.

Love is the greatest gain – don't miss out on it.

———•●•———

And God is everything.
That having been said. . . let's play.

———•●•———

Every moment is a joyous occasion, so shine with that
radiance and love that you are.

———•●•———

Bring beautiful harmonies and melodies
to awaken the sleeping mind.

———•●•———

My prayer is Love

LET ME

Let me touch you deeply
Let me love you easily
Let me know you completely.

Let me breathe you with my inhale
Let me love you with my exhale
Let me hold you with my joy
Let me caress you with my smile.

Let me enter your kingdom of love –
and let's rest in the heart's moment
in that beautiful Garden of Eden.
Close your eyes, and in solitude –
a distance away, I am with you…
right within you…in your kingdom of joy –
in your bed of peace, in your love of life –
I am with you!

MOTHER TIERRA[1]

I want to submerge and bury myself under mother's blanket of soil, and let her children care and tend to me in the finest of matter as if one of their brood. And I would let their feet, antennas, and legs pamper me and rock me back and forth in their diligent care.

And above, the flowers would grow and I would reach and touch their roots and hear their song and feel the sunshine and hear the birds sing. I would roll through mother's tunnels and find the water streams below, and let them bathe and shower me with full massage and like a log transverse in gentle glide through the caves and hallways to corridors of her underworld.

Oh, how beautiful and peaceful to bury myself deep below and be settled in her bosom and soothed by her heartbeat. Oh madre tierra, te quiero – te quiero[2]!

—•—

I am you in ways that you
know you are me. Our
souls within our hearts' door
are united, and pleased they
are to meet again.

---

[1] *Tierra*: Spanish for "Earth."

[2] *Te quiero*: Spanish for "I love you" (non-literal translation).

I love this moment –
With me
Here in it

———•●•———

Enlighten me with the words of your soul
so that I may write upon your heart
the depth of my love

Brighten me with the touch of your Spirit
so that I may awaken the truth
upon every sense of my Being

———•●•———

Engulf yourself in a cocoon of love –
a total encompassing love –
a calm, settled passion
for the moment's love.

———•●•———

There is only joy from which to drink,
the rest is pure life in action.

Let's take this circle of love
and work it amongst us.

—·•·—

Thanksgiving

May the birds of wisdom fly beneath you
and lift you to joyous moments as we ponder
the marvelous gifts bestowed upon us

Give thanks to every breath
of creation we give and receive

May love fill your every wish
and may the token of happiness
enter your thoughts in every moment

—·•·—

Surround me with your Beauty,
Touch me with your Grace,
Fill me with your Joy.

PAGES OF MY LIFE

I want to be a poem of love where every line between me is a story.

> I want to be the words that flow endlessly through
> the pages of my life,
> where every breath is a rhyme.

I want to be a letter of joy where my words are of love and the message of it brings simple tears of joy and satisfaction to the heart.

> I want to be the music that sings and I want to be
> the flower within my heart.

And to be the stream that flows in-between my dreams so as to keep alive the dreams within the dream.

I want to be the honesty that keeps the light bright, that shines with aptitude and attitude.

> I want to slowly die.

I want to be the everlasting word that never fails
and the pillar that reaches to the top,
and I want to gently sit upon the clouds that bring the shade
and be the rainbow that clears the way.

> Yes, that's the way I would like to be if anything at all is
> set in me.

OPEN BOOK

I am an open book of love.
Tell me not to speak, and I will speak of love.

Surround me with the winds of fire,
and I will open the way.

Touch me, and I am.
Breathe me and I live.

Tell me the story of the time we were united in One,
and I will bring castles of joy to thee.

I open to the streams within me —
and come to sense that I am everything
and thus free of all.

—————— • • • ——————

Keep the love and joy
        a happy flame within the heart.

We are each a beautiful flower
in God's garden of love.
Even the weeds are caressed by the winds
and they are showered by the rains,
as they too are medicine upon the hearts of men.

Shine!
Shine, my pretty stem, my glorious bloom,
and stand tall and sway to the joy
and the song of life and cherish your place
upon the soil that you grow from.

———•———

Motivate yourself by love

———•———

There are only a few things worthwhile seeing
and that is love, joy, and peace.

Find these gems in-between your daily breaths.

<u>Red Cabbage Meal</u>

Thank you hands that feed the earth the seeds to our delicious red cabbage. Thank you cabbage for your growth and cycle of life given to the universe. Thank you my hands for gently cutting and savoring with the heart a loving meal. Thank you tomato, olive oil and onions for your part, for your march to a rhythm that brings flavor and a wholesome dish to the table.

———·•·———

Are you a lover in love with life?

———·•·———

You are joy
You are peace
Live it

The greatest story ever told -
    The greatest story ever written,
    The greatest story ever lived -
        Is a love story...
            Your story of love.

Venus

See her. Now look upon Venus and know that she shines so brightly because of her harmony and balance. Know, that upon her are Beings of enormous depth, understanding and encompassing love. Now, be aware that you are connected energetically to the center of the earth and to the universe. Activate this connection by imagining and feeling a pure white love light emanating from your feet to the center of the earth. Imagine and feel a pure white love light reaching from the top of your head out into the universe. Next, bring these two love and joy filled lights and meet them in your heart.

Now, once more look at Venus and breathe in and out. Send your awareness that you know that upon her reside Beings of love. Ask them to show you patience and to show you how to incorporate this total encompassing love in you so that you may project it and be it. Ask them to teach you and share with you their knowledge. Feel her, become her, send your love, and receive her love, all with conscious movement of breath.

—•—

It's a beautiful moment

I am loving your presence in my life.

———·•·———

Love is a practice…
  Of looking deeply…
    Not just the intention –
      But love is action.

———·•·———

Understanding is an essence of loving.

———·•·———

Love is seeing God
and making him your friend

I Am in Love

There is no greater song than the music of the lovers.
I am my beloved and my beloved is mine is where
peace resides. No other realm has the capacity to
imitate the steps of love. Only the selves in us and beside us
can achieve peace.

I am in Love

And only the worlds beneath me can attest to this rhythm of
truth. And the worlds high above foresee the spectrum of truth
that is within me. The music of love creates the song of inner
peace.

This is Love. This is Peace.

Together among the leaves of gold written upon the altar, there,
the scent and the breath of Saints release the music of glorious
vision of combined love. This is what the world is waiting on.
This is what the masters have brought and now the prophecy
sustains the truth in balance.

I am to be dictated upon paper with the scent of breath upon
the pages racing to sustain the glory.

There is another breath to take, another song to sing, another
place to be, another world to see, to claim and to reign.

The Peace becomes the piece to surrender to this infinite love
breath, and I joyously become the ultimate lover of love, of joy,
and we are placed among the celestial kings.

I am in Love

I Am Missing Your Presence

My heart looks forward to when I see you again.
Meanwhile, I take deep breaths and I close my eyes, and
I call upon your essence and I feel you. And my heart
warms up with our love. You are precious, you are joy,
and you are a sparkle and an Angel in my life.

I love you.

———•———

I love you. Yes, I do.
I may not know you, yet I see.
I send my love to you.
Take it and blanket yourself with my warmth
as I rock you back and forth.
Feel the expression that I do care about you,
and even more that I understand you.

A gentle back and forth, a gentle caress,
these are my actions for you.
Take my love and embrace it around you.
Embrace my love, breath in my love.
It is eternal and I want you to know
all is and will be well.

I feel a tremendous love
and I want to caress you
like the angels do.
It is a potent,
totally encompassing
love that I feel
and I want to mesh
and become One with you
as my every cell wants
to meet your every Self.

———•———

I am your beloved –
   Kiss me so that I may enter
      into the realm of the loved.

PURE LOVE

It is not protective love
It is not motherly love
It is not fatherly love
It is not admiration
It is not attraction
It is not limited by action
It is not fooled by guilt
It is not surrounded by anguish
It is not worrisome love
It is not instinctive love –
Nor the love of a child,
or love of a husband or wife
or a dearly beloved.
It is love with a farther reach,
encompassing a whole individual –
loving the whole in spite of its parts,
its segments – words, actions, attitudes, personality.
Even beyond character or morale.

—·•·—

Love is the answer.
But you can't get
To the answer until
You experience the love.

The Artist In Me

Sometimes I want to use no brush and my hand wants to be the sole instrument to paint. Sometimes my heart wants to leap and embrace the canvas of Life. Sometimes my heart is in repose and the body wants to sit back and observe all the painted canvases, mine and others. Sometimes my mind works to adjust this and that. And sometimes it just wants to sit back and smile and be a happy mind.

At times my hands enjoy the splashing, erratic, rough brushstrokes mounted haphazardly and lovingly across time and space. Sometimes a delicate smooth, gentle stroke is called for. Many times I am pleased, other times I act pleased. It's the knowing that the art is the art, sometimes more, sometimes less, that makes me sign each piece as author unknown. When the instrument is the body, I sign with author known. Otherwise my name is all the names, that when added up become no name. Such is the business of the art of life.

And this business of the living art can get complicated. Too many agents, too many eyes, and I's, all dictating how the piece should feel, should act, should think. I – well I just mind my own business of art – and I let no one pressure or dictate my colors or strokes. Sometimes I take heed on the advice on brushes to use and upon which canvas to paint and I may latch on to an idea given – but then the toy is mine, and I play with juicy enthusiasm bending here and there, curving this and that – molding past here – and touching off there.

It may not look like much when done – but oh – the aliveness of the eyes within each cell of me can be no greater in response than when I play in God's art studio of life. No matter rain, sunshine, storm or earthquake, I am there dancing to the art of mine – that I so lovingly create with all the toys and splendid colors I reach out for and are given to me.

Be a beacon of light and love,
showing the way for me and others.

—·•·—

May the waters wash the gems to their brilliance.
May the sun announce its triumph in your heart,
May She, Mother Earth, rock you gently in peace,
and may the title of joy reign
in your Kingdom.

—·•·—

MAY THE PIECE THAT YOU SEEK
BE THAT OF LOVE

The One

The Separate

The Chaos

The Beautiful

*L*ife is beautiful no matter the steps taken.

———•—

It is necessary to understand and see the value of separateness in order to see and understand the value of unity. So we have taken the strands of light and dismantled them in all kinds of separateness throughout the years and surely we are now assembling those bands of light again.

———•—

You have to feel the separateness to feel the unity.
You have to be the separateness to be the unity.

———•—

OUR IDEAL: To align our words, thoughts and vision with our actions, so as to become One in purpose.

———•—

We are all beautiful children.
It's getting along that gets complicated.

The concept, the power, the creation and space of being in the eye of the storm. It is also being within the drum, listening and being part of the beat. The music and swaying and dancing to it from the waist up. The feet are grounded and centered, focused on where it stands and keeping an eye on the storm and placing oneself in the middle. Eventually you do not move and all around you creates the center for you.

Ah – life is beautiful.

———•—

We are all One – you understand it.
You know it. Practice it.
Believe it even in the
non-sense of not believing.

———•—

Safe to conclude at this point that we have broken down all items of thought into smaller compartments, in order to understand and complete a larger picture. A given necessity to understand the complexity of breaking down to simplistic form, to go back up and address the whole as many compartments of the One.

The Kingdom of God
is not exclusive.

It is not selective
in its members.

WE NEED THE LIGHT to see the darkness – we need the darkness to see the light. They are not enemies, they are friends, and they walk hand in hand. They dance to the music of Life.

Why child, do you continue to believe that one is evil? In doing so, are not both evil? In doing so has the Creator not created evil? Then perhaps, it is the child, being the children we are, that in its play, has created the demons and with time has grown to believe they are real?

———·●·———

We need to record the experience of separateness to understand interconnectivity and to further the understanding of the One.

———·●·———

Everything is a duality at this level of life studies. We have even made God a duality.

HEART/MIND, FEMALE/MALE, LIGHT/DARK

....This new spiritual birth that I speak about, the changes to come have to do with the Female and Male energies and their current activities. You see, with the new Spiritual Birth upon us, that birth entails a new relationship between Male/Female energies.

Some of you have heard of the Kundalini energy that resides within us. When awakened, it travels from the base of the spine up through the top of the spine. In addition, this Kundalini energy is present within each organ and system within our body, and furthermore, within each cell. Further out, this Kundalini energy exists within each city, each nation, each continent, and planet Earth. Further still, our planetary system has this Kundalini force and so does the Milky Way, and so on and so on.

This force is what makes up movement. This movement equals force, which equals change. That movement is the rising of the Female aspect within Kundalini, which is in itself a Female force. So what do I speak of here? I speak of the building blocks within all which are two energies, which is the dance of two forces, Male and Female. It's two strands of energies dancing, revolving side by side, as you see in a DNA helix. It's the Female/Male energy who together rise in the Kundalini force.

So the force surging through at this moment is the rediscovery of the Female energy, understanding its place, and understanding its role in nature. So let's look at this force that is now rising within each of us, on Earth and in our solar system and beyond.

First, let's understand the role that each aspect of Kundalini plays. The Female, that is now requesting that we acknowledge, accept and understand her, that is birthing upward to bring us her knowledge and to assist us through our delivery into the next world – She is the Creator, the Matrix. She sets the rules and determines the arena, the playing field.

You can say that when someone dies – physically leaves this world – the She Force has determined and changed that individual's playing field, arena. She is the Queen and is represented on the left side of your body. Anytime you have issues with the left side of the body, it is the She aspect.

The Male aspect of Kundalini, that which has exhibited the major force within our current history, that force now requests that we understand his loving partner with whom he dances the night away. He determines the moves within the playing field set by Her. He indicates to us the direction, the steps to take in this dance of life. He is the King and is found on the right side of the body. Again, any dis-ease, pain, problems on the right side of the body corresponds to the male aspect. Remember though, there is further breakdown/division going inward...that is within each organ, system, and cell, each have their own Kundalini with both Male and Female aspects. This applies further out from us as well.

So here we are! Today, we are being shown the playing field. She has created our new arena, He has indicated our path – the way – the moves within the game board established by Her. The new way, the New World – what is to come will have these two aspects of Light in their respective order. She on the left – creator, and He on the right-side of the Father, and the child in the middle. And guess who is the child? Yes, you and I!

How awesome and beautiful the child that understands and thus obeys. The Child looks to the left and sees Mother and knows the playing field and arena that he must work within. The Child smiles in knowing its boundaries have been set.

The Child looks to the Right and sees Father, and he knows the moves to make, and he smiles in joy and peace for this guidance. The Child knows and understands that he who sits at the right hand of the Father, not only knows the moves, but also the arena. He knows Her intimately. He understands the Left side. The Child now sees that they – mother/father – are One. Not separate anymore.

The New World is established – a kingdom where Male-Female are viewed as One, working together in sync. Our will then becomes His will. The Queen is now in her rightful place, the King continues in his rightful place, and the Prince/Princess now knows his/her true place.

Alright...so let's get back to the Heart and Mind. What do we listen to? For a long time we've only been listening to the Father aspect of the Heart, and only the Father aspect of the Mind. But here now, Mother comes into the picture. We now hear her voice and Father says – Listen! Viewing the total physical body, the Male aspect is represented by the Heart. This may surprise you, but it is so. All along in our past history we have been listening to our Heart and its passions. But now we have to go further – we are being asked to seek. And so we go into the Heart and listen to that other aspect that resides there – the Female voice. Merging these two energies, Male/Female, gives you the rising Kundalini within the Heart and the Heart becomes in love and alive.

Now the Mind. Looking at the total physical body, the Mind is Female. Within the Mind, when we look further, we find its partner the divine Male force. When we unite these two there is passion. There is love, understanding and knowledge.

All have both Male and Female aspects. Our work is to open the doors within the Heart and Mind so that both are in balance, in their rightful place, in a state of peace and love. The Child – you and I balanced in the middle – becomes the new Creator. This is what changes our complete Being, our species, and elevates us to what we are to become.

I would love to chat more with you about what you bring
to the table of knowledge; there is confusion among us –
the belief that spirituality and that God are the way
through the heart alone. Yet we act without our spouse
in this equation, that delightful Mind with which He is
enamored. And He does not desire that we leave Her, the
Mind, out of His embrace. The female energy, the She that
she is, brings Him into our hearts in complete union to the
whole that we are.

———•———

I am the soul that encompasses and divides

———•———

BE SEPARATE

Be your uniqueness; be the same as the other.
Be your oneness with all;
be the separateness that you are.

It's trying, trying to understand,
implement and be this balance
between the poles of all that we are.

In the end, march to your own tune and beat,
yet follow the higher beat to Life.

As children we grow up and learn and become aware that good and bad have the same ingredients. Thus, good and bad become an opinion, an understanding depending on whose team or side you are on.

—·•·—

God's hand is in everything

—·•·—

**I entered sacred time/space
and I realized that the "I" has become obsolete.**

—·•·—

*Spirituality is the result of scientific investigation +
mathematical calculation + religious exploration;*

Spirituality can be called the unity of the sciences into one main stream of consciousness that encompasses the understanding that all sciences, all mathematical equations and all religions protrude as one cohesive band of unity - instead of separate unrelated warring factions.

ROOTED SOLIDLY TO A BELIEF IS ADMIRABLE

These times and the moments to come can be particularly difficult to accept, to master the lesson, to comprehend, to move to the next grade level, for those who are firmly attached to a particular religion without flexibility of movement. Rooted solidly to a belief is admirable and has its place. Being unable to bend with the winds from the root up can topple the tree and even break it in half. Bending like bamboo to the winds of life, provides compact and solid mobility within the currents and flow of Life. Are you so fixed in your religious beliefs set by the Sons of Man? If so, there is much to learn, to review and to clarify in this area. It is time to repair and build upon the cracking foundation.

Begin to understand that the Sons of Man are but children, and as such they do as children do. The child embellishes the story for they know not as of yet that the made-up reality outside their head is separate from the made-up reality inside their head. And as such, because of this confusion, which is a natural process in a child, the stories change, and are told from a child's perspective.

So what do we do if we evaluate ourselves and find we are locked quite rigidly in our domesticated, taught and learned religion beliefs? We awaken the aspect of The Son of God within us. You see, we are made up of both aspects.

Listen, for The Son of God is awakening
from his slumber.

IN THE DIVIDING, it was given so that we may dissect and learn and see the layers, the workings and the parts of the One. The children of the earth have taken the curriculum of dividing and separating and have focused on the difference and have applied the mathematical value of less and then translated it to inferior. The purpose of the separation, the division, is to get to know the parts intimately, to understand their uniqueness, their particular characteristics and function. And then to view its opposite equation, addition, as the coming together and seeing how all the ingredients and pieces of the puzzle add up to create one beautiful picture. And in understanding the parts, we understand the whole. Until we understand the parts and that none are inferior, but all have their place and purpose, addition will be hard to master.

———•—

We need to be grounded in the experience of unity.

———•—

Together, we form one bond
that unites us through and into eternity.

———•—

I have been of
no name, no nation, no religion, no status, no words.

Expand your thought in the view of what the contents of the word *beautiful* encompasses.

———·•·———

LIFE IS A RELIGIOUS SCIENCE. And we are moving closer to understanding that all religions, all philosophies, and all of science is but one expression viewed through a parting lens. We are coming to the times where this will be understood completely and simply without much fanfare...other than the occasional demise of feeling torn apart, alliance to one quadrant of a belief system, or the superiority of one aspect at the expense of another.

———·•·———

All myths become **One**
All religions become **One**
All sciences become **One**
All aspects integrate

The animal kingdom is understood as **One**
The law – for every action there is an equal
reaction – is understood to affect the **One**

Science and religion will be seen as One. Start now to see them as One. At the upper levels, at the core they are one and the same. Only at the lower levels the necessity to understand them and see them in their own self created separate light.

———•———

It is through the separating, the division, the dissection – that we understand the mechanics – the components – and in understanding the components and the mechanics we understand the whole.

———•———

It is only in the separating
that you can unite.

———•———

Who are we? We are all and everything.
There is nothing we have not been or done.

A tumbling weed swaying back and forth to the current of the winds with a request to steer a buffalo head has appeared.

Graze me with patience, a calm sea and love.
Cradle me with a lullaby song near the heart between your arms.

*H*old my face with the caress of your hand.
Smooth out the tension with your fingers of creation.

In the cold I want to be held.
The steam of my purpose has suddenly become of no matter.

No longer am I the One.

— • —

*I am in everything and
everything is in me.*

The Peace Piece

I.   I have taken the gun and shot the head,
I have taken the bow and speared the heart.
I have likened the image and seen who I am
I have spoken the word and heard who I was.
I have breathed once and suffered much.
I have become the pieces of written time, of scattered
moments.
I have seen the bridges among time and space,
        and now I am.

We are drums of dance and prayer throughout the ages,
the music of all the ears.
We have come to sing of the glory through the chords of
all peoples.
There is distinction of breath
between yours and mine.
I hold my breath and you become, and only as much as
breath can hold.
Then it circulates among the nostrils of the One,
ready to pounce its breath with strength and playfulness
where it breathes the scent of love, and knows of no
other scent...
Hold. . .
Hold. . .
Hold. . .
        And it pounces its breath with strength and
                playfulness back to me.
        I breathe in the scent of love as much as
                breath can hold.

II.   I have lived all the times and all the ages.
I have swept the floors, climbed the stairs, crossed the rivers and tiptoed through the ages.
There is no place I have not lived, no time I have not moved, no place I have not seen, no time I have not visited.
      I have been there.

I have seen the mighty wars, the persecution, the anguish, the prophets, the healers, the lepers – all for love have I been. No other.
I am all the tyrannies, all the gold.
I am all the genocides, all the rebuilt,
all the torn. I am experienced by nature and self by love.
I come between the worlds of light and dark as a shade of hues speaking of the continuous flow and stream and current within me.

I am no other, than encompassing totality
between the thighs of ecstasy and receiving,
folding, releasing in the tight dance of love,

Summoning the lords of breath to light the fire
among my earth, igniting the gates of
eternal mind to open and flush me with
ardent communion among the all that I am.

Breathe. Beat. Hear.
There is music in my heart.

III.   There is more than one breath to breathe, more than one
        entering and arriving.
        It calls with eagerness and excitement and dances with
        the swirl of the lush of springtime.
        Embraced in the songs of eternity fulfilling the
        expansion and birth of the beginning and entering the
        opening of eternity.
        I am all the worlds, all the times, all the ages.
        I am the darkness and I am the light.
        I am the mountains and the rivers.
        I am the spoils and the fruit.

        I have traced the scent of the accused and the accuser,
        the savior and the killer, the lamb and the wolf.
        I have been pierced, stabbed, and shot.
        I have struck, disassembled and destroyed.
        I have swung the sword, yielded the harpoon, flung the
        arrow, hung the sword in agony.
        I have cried, laughed, and pierced the records of life
        with my anguish, pain and joy.

        There is nothing I have not done to myself, as outside of
        me is all that I am.
        There is no joy I have not brought to myself that outside
        of me is there.
        We are parallel universes, sharing space, time and joy,
        progressing in song, in harmony, towards the beginning
        of the ages,
        remembering the sweet music, dancing the movement of
        all times.
        Push, pull.
        In, out. . .
        And all is well.

IV.   I am breath that augments with each breath.
I am fire that extinguishes fire.
I am water that runs through my veins.
In union with breath we extinguish the fire.
I am the stone built as the altar.
I am the union of breath and water that nourishes the fire.
I am the pigeon that dies, the anchor that is gone, the pottery that is shattered, the dress that is tight.

I am the vomit of life cleansing the soul.
I am the message, and the bringer of light.
I prepare, I set aside, I bring in, I construct and destruct.
I have the news, the title and the song.
I am the food, water and fresh breeze.
I am the puzzle of pieces,
I pick up where I left off and continue where I ended.
      I am the peace of ecstasy
      and the ecstasy of peace
            I have been in every place and
            in-between.

V.   I have been all faiths, all religions, all dogmas and all beliefs.
I have stood tall and proud,
fallen and beaten.
I have won the battles and cursed the names.
There is no title of emotion I have not lived,
no plant I have not seen, no animal I have not heard, no ocean I have not crossed, no song I have not sung.
All have been recited, all lived, breathed, felt by every ounce of the core of my heart.
I have written of all the times,
I have been placed between the pages of
every book.

I breathe and the universe breathes with me.
I exhale and the universe exhales with me.
I cry and the universe cries with me.
I laugh and the universe laughs with me.
I praise and the universe praises with me.

I am not alone.

VI.   I have been all the change, every march, every torture, every song, every piece of music, every beat of drum.
I am the tempest, the storm, the pressure.
I secure all your insecurities and devour them with pleasure.
I lick the endless times of pain and secure a blanket net around you.
I've been there and everywhere, in-between the pain and suffering, in-between the stories and among the stories.
       There I rest.

None escapes me.

Every shout I have heard, every stumble I have felt, each new birth I have witnessed, each autumn dance I have seen. Each character I have assembled and disassembled, each breath I have taken has indeed been agreed, nothing lost, nothing gained, only simple calculations misunderstood through the times, that the lights emanations equal One.

I have been every science, every discovery, every specimen, every breath, every thought, every word. . .
All understood and misunderstood
       and yet I stand.

VII.   I have been an atheist, a sorcerer, a monk, a Jew and a Catholic. I have been poor beyond means, and rich beyond imagination.
I have sat Below and Above,
And yet I claim no land.
I was the lie and the truth and now I sit between them.
I have been the words that deceive, hurt and sting.
I have spoken the breath that comes and soothes and stands firm in pace and beat.

Having been through each hole and crevice, untouched, unscathed by the light, side by side I roam inside turned sour by the news.

I lay me down and let the pain subside. I've just released
an ache, nothing less, nothing more than what I am.

The bearer of the news has always been me. Disguised
by stories here and there. In disguise I am sent from one
story to another.
There is no difference between who I am and who you
are.
       I feel solemn, contemplative.

VIII.   I've been the slime, the slum and the parasite.
I've eaten the rat, the corpse and the weak.
I've infested the deer, brought down the sublime,
insisted on chaos, demanded a voice – so here I am in
full attire
awaiting, speaking my past future.
I've been the wicked and the damned,
The exploited and the tarnished,
Nailed down and glued and raptured from the night.
I am the angel of death that prays for your recovery,
The attic of love that begs to be released,
The tormented who seeks shelter,
The space that wants to reunite.

Why do you fear me still? Why do you taunt me and
remove yourself from where I embrace and hold our
love churning in unison breath to the applaud of the
cherubs?

       I've been speaking it all the time –
       you have not been listening.
       I've been here all the time –
       you've not seen me.
       I have been awake, you asleep.
       I have been everywhere and
       in-between.

WE ARE ALL EQUAL in the essence of who we are. We compliment with our extraordinariness and unique and forthright Selves that make us separate. Enjoy and bring the separateness forward as a gift to God. Enjoy and cherish the Oneness of all.

———·•·———

As we move to understand the concept of Oneness, each individual total Being combination will require specific and unique needs as opposed to "same for all" or "one fits all."

———·•·———

The reality of the Oneness is as solid as the reality of the separateness.

———·•·———

There is no action we have not done or thought we have not thought.

PRAYER 1

We are One.
We are joyous.
We are eternal.
We are forgiving of all.

Bring us the flame to twist upon
the emblem of our hearts,
as we place the altar upon the footsteps
taken by man.

We are joyous.
We are One.
Bring us the eternal flame to place around us
as we move together to new heights.

———·●·———

THE PEACE WITHIN EACH
PIECE OF THE PUZZLE
BRINGS PEACE TO THE WHOLE WORLD

Fear
&
Anger

Pierce the veil of fear and enter its domain. Reside within the sacred heart and know your journey is among all men of Knowledge. Comfort your repose, as you sit at the center of God. Balance the equanimity and you will know who you are.

———•●•———

We must consult our fears,
our hopes and our dreams.

———•●•———

We can no longer turn our face away
from the great teachings of anger and of fear.

———•●•———

Take your challenges and encounters with fear and delve into it and work with it. Get to know it. What is it? Greet it. Taste it. Smell it. Adjust it. Sample it. View it. Feel it.

I want to create, not out of anger, but out of love. Not because I dislike anger, not at all indeed, as she and I have become good friends. I just rather make the decisions of my moments under the influence of pure love.

— ·•· —

Our fears are a measuring tool to diagnose where we are in our knowledge and our learning.

— ·•· —

We are afraid of knowledge.
We are afraid it will be used against us,
either by others or by ourselves.

— ·•· —

Are you closing doors of opportunity
with the misunderstanding of
anger, jealousy or fear?

Most of us are afraid of dying –
but the truth is
we are afraid of living.

ANGER IS A CLUE –

A MESSENGER OF FORGIVENESS. IT IS THE ANNOUNCER AT THE GATE OF CHOICE THAT SOMETHING IS INCOMPLETE.

—·●·—

What I went through in my initiation – a birth on one level – I was not afraid. On another level, I touched and experienced the depths and dungeons of fear, the result being the reconciliation of God/evil.

—·●·—

Be true to yourself. Accept and work your fears,
pain, love, joys, regrets, obstacles,
and highs with due respect.

—·●·—

I find most of us have a challenge with trusting life, trusting our helpers and guides on a higher level, and even ourselves and God.

Ah, anger – she is my friend.
I try to tame her, but she relents no less
than I forego of my love.
Tightly held, we embrace each other
and dance to our solo parts.
Ah - she thinks she can pull me apart –
I think I can pull her together.

Don't tell her I told you so, even though she knows –
She wishes she could dominate me,
I wish she would not bother me.
So when she comes
I feel her breath of fire
and her face of force.
I relent to her expression.
I let her touch me and we become One.

I accommodate to her wishes,
she expresses the anger – trying to tell me –
"Listen, there is more here to know."
I enter breath, light, calm, kindness, and common sense.
Slowly and surely, I see the guidance
of what she wants to show.
Eventually I understand her unspoken words,
her force of fire, and realize the wisdom of her heat.
And so, in time, we dance to another tune, and it's love
that churns out, and anger – she departs.

$\mathcal{D}$espair

> can build the most gorgeous solid construction. The depths of fear can build the strongest and most firm foundation. The ravages of anger can build the most beautiful of calm notions and understanding.

—·•·—

Entering the dark beautiful abyss
can bring the knowledge of love.

—·•·—

I t truly is a beautiful world. We have just misplaced it to a place most people believe is necessary for the research. We need not do this type of research. It is too painful, constrictive, failing, accosting, and tumultuous. We need to slide to the side to face its opposite bravely - and say no to the constant enjoyment of living the emotional tides, waves and bumps into the shore. Instead, ride smooth sails and deliver quiet states of Being. Search for what is there instead of searching to create what is not there.

I don't want to be
invisible anymore. I want
to be visible
and I'm not afraid!

Pain loosens up the made up rules
that chain us to our everyday life.

— ·•· —

Anger needs to be fused with love.

— ·•· —

What are you afraid of?
I am afraid of fear.

— ·•· —

FEAR AND ANGER are surging strongly.
How do we handle it?

With a welcoming sign, understanding that on a higher
level they are here to assist us in our development, our
growth and our birth.

Afraid to look over the edge? Invite fear in.
Tell it, "Come on in!"

———·●·——

That which you fear of the light will *retract*.
That which you fear of the dark will *attract*.

———·●·——

Avoid the fear of the process...
the resistance to become the change.

Release the pain,
Enter the way,
Remove the veil,
Replace the curtain.

———·●·——

My experience has been that behind evil, there tends to be a key ingredient and that is fear masquerading in various outfits; fear of abandonment, not being loved, not having, not getting, fear of hunger, fear of loss, of love, fear of the past, repeating the past, fear of the future, fear of the unseen, fear of repercussion, of punishment, of pain, fear of death, fear of living, fear of knowledge, fear of God, fear of losing, of winning, fear of the dark, fear of the light, fear of fear itself - thus becoming fearful of ourselves and others. So we are afraid of life and even more afraid of God.

I Am

Some strokes are angry, some angelic.
The way, the rhythm – they all have their place
because without the turbulence of the sea –
the ferocity of the oceans – I would not come to be.

I am, I am, I am
but a speck rising up and down the mind of the
ways of this sea where minds meet to battle, rage, and
merge with the undercurrents that swiftly
submerge us and take us to new consciousness.

The sea of emotions are vast.
Cast out upon my soul I write the rhythms
of my strokes painted on the canvas of time.

I am, I am, the calm of the waters,
the breath of the sea.

I am, I am, this rest beneath me.

WHAT ARE WE AFRAID OF? Of love, true love? If we were to feel true Divine Love right now, all would stop for us as we could not continue to be how we act, how we see ourselves, nor see others, nor continue to act towards others in the same manner…once the depth of the Christ/Divine conscious love is felt within the heart.

———·•·———

There is absolutely nothing to fear
not even fear itself

———·•·———

The forces are now such that we are being encouraged and pushed to exercise our emotional body. This means the energies are present to bring forth the opportunities to encounter our various emotional states – fear and anger being the primary leaders in assisting us to open ourselves up to our Selves. We must experience and feel intensely to rapture through to our Higher Self.

———·•·———

WOULD YOU NOT TRADE THIS PIECE OF FEAR FOR PEACE OF MIND?

Knowledge

We are all afraid of knowledge for we fear
it will be used against us.

———·●·———

We are moving up the ladder of knowledge

———·●·———

The higher up in vibration –
the less we will need to eat, drink and sleep.

———·●·———

As we move up the line of Knowledge – previous
information, facts and knowledge are no longer accurate
or correct. They become undone in the face of the new
knowledge.

THE MORE I EXPERIENCE, the more all is real. The more all is quite secure in its existence, if even for a moment. Just because a move upward brings in a change to newer laws and makes something from before non-existent, it does not mean it was not real. Just because one may experience the sudden movements through different segments and movements of time, for me, instead of nullifying the reality experienced, it magnifies that all is alive and real.

—•—

Thanking our guides, angels,
counsel and advisors of the upper realms...

ASSUMPTION: these realms are all-knowing
with proper and correct emotion.

In fact these realms are in evolution just as we are.
They make mistakes and errors of which they learn just
like we do. They too do their best at each moment
and knowing that brings peace to the soul.

Recall child – the realm of the newborn and infant. It is important to remember their realm – as we fault in thinking their realm is the same as the realm of the adult. The newborn and infant has to develop subtle exterior parts of the Self, and as such does not have the proper build to be among much movement, sound, people, activity and noise upon birth. I've seen newborns in grocery stores and among crowds, infants around six months old at major swim meets and at various other events that are loud and of much action, movement and noise. A slow and gradual introduction to the infant's new world is best. The child is aware of the finest of movement and subtlest of noise that you have forgotten. Recall, so as to not further debilitate the child's development. To the infant, our daily routines and social encounters are overwhelming. Do not push to accommodate man's time upon the infant. Easy does it. Instead, introduce your child slowly upon this world so as to allow nature's time to develop properly and firmly the various subtle bodies of the child. Remember – recall.

—•—

As much as I encourage the importance to seek
the knowledge, imagination is higher in purpose.

Knowledge changes with each step you take
up the ladder of Life.

Imagination creates and expands on the knowledge.

There is more to the mind
than what we are aware of.

Know there is more to emotions
than what we perceive.

And there is more to the physical body
than what we can imagine.

—·•·—

What if there are things faster than light?

—·•·—

Cancer is an internal struggle manifested
in the physical as an agreement to go to war.

—·•·—

I closed my eyes and in my mind's eye I saw $E=mc^2$ as if suspended in space/time. And to the right of the equation both in front of and towards the back were two other equations, each in its own dimension of time, that I understood complemented and gave a distinct completeness and connectedness to the entire equation and that it was all simply one equation. The implications being that of time and related to movement of time.

INCOMPREHENSIBLE MAGNITUDE

Imagine if you will, that our universe is both finite and infinite. What if our universe is finite in the sense that the edge of this grand universe is contained within a lining sac of sorts, and it separates our grand universe from other grand universes that we don't even realize exist. And these other grand universes are also contained within a lining sac that separates one grand universe from another ... and another ... and another ... and another grand universe. Here we find the infinite aspect of the universe. We will come to know some day, of all these grand universes contained within a sac of sorts, separated from one another yet operating as one incomprehensible immense complete Universe[1].

———•———

We will know that life is abundant beyond what we currently believe or think, not only on our Earth but also in our Solar System, in our Milky Way, in our galaxy and in our universe. It is beyond our current cognitive skills and ability, to comprehend this complete and full spectrum of Life. Beings, many Beings, at different levels of knowledge, development, functions and different physical vehicles exist.

---

[1] **Universe**: Written with a capital U, Universe encompasses more than one "universe." As of now, incomprehensible, as we have not even understood the circumference of our universe, much less can we perceive the universes that are beyond it, nor the One Universe.

THERE IS NO SUCH THING AS RACISM at the higher levels, as the light has purified and narrowed its lens' view through only the One eye and has bared the word and concept of racism to its root.

At this level what does exist is the inborn power over another.

My child, it does not matter the skin color, religion, social status, nation where you were born, sex, age, color of your eyes, or how you dress. These are just dressings to clothe and disguise the look of your eyes upon the reality of who we are...

> by nature, inclined to savor the desire to take power over another, and in the perfect precise squeeze of a moment, by choice - we may steer to do it - no matter the dressing of another.

———•●•———

We are starved for knowledge –
each cell and Self within cries for the knowing.
Feed it the knowledge!

Some traditions, some primal, animal instinctive energies are meant to be kept, continued, and used to build our solid foundation for growth. Other certain traditions and certain primal energies need to be revisited, cleared, transformed, and elevated in concept. They no longer serve, apply, or benefit our mental or emotional intelligence, need, or heightened sensitivity that we are developing at these times.

An example of traditions that need to be overcome would be: the tradition of the bull fight, be it religious in nature or otherwise; the tradition of cornering and gathering of lives of our brethren the dolphin, seals, and whales by many nations. An example of an energy that needs to be overcome is the fervent, primal, instinctive energy to reproduce. This energy needs to be understood at its cellular level – both metaphysically and physically. And we need to upgrade its version of instinct for survival, manage its pressure, and clear its distortions. This topic of reproduction, of sexuality, is a whole book in and of itself. Nonetheless, we are behind in our studies in regard to this vital, unequaled, majestic energy and we have much to catch up on.

———•———

We use knowledge as a weapon and thus we as a nation have become afraid of knowledge because we think it will be used against us.

It has been my experience that time is very real. You can even get to levels where you can enter a vacuum of stillness and where you can manage the controls to speed up, reverse, or move forward into different movements of time.

—·•·—

TIME: A movement of light whose speed of light is determined by vibration.

—·•·—

Speed of time determines the glueness of the material worlds.

—·•·—

Some things are hard to hear or believe.

One of them is that every action within our history is in order. Nothing is out of place. There is a lesson in every event, and the movement of emotions is essential to our learning and to our progress up the ladder of maturity.

What if there have been many "Big Bangs" that have a cycle that looks like this:

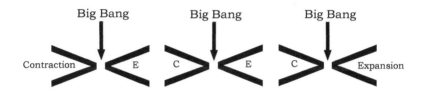

————•●•———

There is more than one light – There is more than one speed of light. Each individual person bears a speed of light within and outside of itself.

————•●•———

Each of you is a transmitter of your knowledge,
not just a receiver.

Not only are we enlightened by the Heavens and the Earth, but we enlighten the Heavens and the Earth.

And in this way we become the Children of Earth that lead the Kingdom into Heaven.

Creation and evolution –
two strands that intertwine
into one fact, one truth –
to show it truly takes two to tango.

———·●·———

There is more than one time, one beat –
there are millions of them.

———·●·———

The key in anything is movement away from ignorance.

———·●·———

GARDEN OF EDEN: We enter this state of unity where the
unawareness of the separateness is not manifested. Stage of
innocence.

FALL OF EDEN: The process by which the knowledge of being
separate within the unity is activated. Stage of self-perception
and self-knowledge.

HEAVEN ON EARTH: The combining of the concept of the
fall of Eden, with the remembrance of interconnectedness
combined with the knowledge of One. Returning to the stage of
innocence coupled with the wisdom of knowledge. Stage of
unity and the Virgin state of pure mind and thoughts.

L ife is a school and not only for you and me – but be aware it is also a school for the angels, for God, for our Higher Self, for our spiritual guides and teachers, for Beings on other solar systems light years ahead in awareness and technology. We are all in movement towards the light of awareness, knowledge, and the movement towards learning. My Egyptian spiritual guides, my animal, plant and rock guides, the Native American Indian guides, all are in a book of learning from Life. They do not know all the answers. They may be better at exacting upon probabilities. Nonetheless, even the highest intent individual here on earth with heart of trust, with joy and comprehension of the love of creation, yet without understanding the specific workings of the knowledge of creation, can open doors, change scripts, write new stories and beginnings that even more evolved and intellectual Beings here on earth or on higher vibrating dimensions are not yet adept at doing.

———•●•———

Accepting:
is in the choosing to open or close the door.

Sound and Sugar

In meeting of prayer with the upper realms I asked, "How and what is the best way for us to attain peace here on earth?" Immediately, I received two words:

1.　　Sound
2.　　Sugar

This question I posed about six years ago and broader and deeper understanding to these answers have slowly been shown to me. Sound is important because through sound we can move and change the configuration and calibration of vibration. This means we can align, balance, and heal aspects of ourselves, our whole Being, and furthermore – planet Earth and other living things through sound. Not only through our efforts of "being green" can we align weather conditions, but more specifically, through the modification of sound it is possible to bring a balance to our weather conditions. Peace in the world begins with each of us. Sound modification, balance, alignment, and peace begins inward and then it is expressed outward of ourselves. This is how we bring peace to our diverse planet – one by one, joining the perpetual light band of Oneness.

Somehow excessive sugar seems to have an amazing effect in distorting and, at times, even blocking certain metaphysical, subtle functions, and communication. If these pathways are distorted, our understanding, knowledge, and even reasoning is distorted. It has taken me six years to understand how even a slightly improper, inaccurate, or excessive amount of sound and sugar can make such an impact on one's balance, alignment, and centeredness. These two aspects have a lot of weight and play in obtaining and maintaining the configuration of the state of peace within us.

Within the Milky Way, we are known as the
Realm of the Children.

———•—

Each planet in our solar system has a consciousness at its center. Mother Earth houses at its center the male Christ energy of the Christ consciousness.

———•—

VISION

The coast of the East of the U.S. will be redirected with a new outline and Florida will resume its complete submersion.

———•—

WE ARE IN AN INTENSE training period right now – in review of a lot of material. No different than anyone studying for a board exam. Take advantage and apply the lessons learned – become the willing student, the passionate student, the student in love with Life and its studies. The student enamored with its material, its courses, its lessons. Bring in the sacred child's sense of awe and wonder, newness and freshness in vision – and the sense of discovery. Touch, feel, hear, smell, sense the essence of being in love with every moment.

Foremost, I am all and everything –
A child scientist dedicated to my studies of exploring and
discovering the world around me.

——— · • · ———

Nutrition:
Knowledge is proper food.

——— · • · ———

There is no better life than the life of a student.
Be a student of life.
Joyful studies!

——— · • · ———

So the myth is changing and as we live the myth, we become
and are the myth.

The mystic stage of the hermit, and of the martyr, need not be employed any longer. That has been done for us, so as to elevate ourselves through a higher process. Take advantage of the stepping stones laid by others through their life, through their experience. You need not become the martyr, nor the hermit, nor the victim, nor the punished, nor the punisher. You need not employ the grieving for what the world is or has become. Your simple need is to establish what all the past has befriended to you, employ its highest capacity in the moment and pursue the goal of the future, for your future. Your future here is not separate from any other's future. So there is no sacrifice to do for tomorrow. There is only the enjoyment of today, the accepting of the flow, letting things be and become, working from within to the outside. We generally seek the order to be from the outside inward. As far as a force and power, it is from within. As far as balance and stability, it is from within, reflecting the outside and bouncing off from the outside. As far as creating and that of change, it is from inside the front brain area and the eyes and the mind inside the body – projected to the outside.

———•———

We are transcending myth and archetypes and we are bringing them to higher levels.

It is the time to enter new terrains and to invest in yourself with money, time, and energy. There is no other way now. The move is upwards towards a shift in our Being. The universe so commands it! Allow yourself to flow within the current of this change. To step aside is to surely prevent transformation. Your metamorphosis will then be different than the intended. So follow the scent. Pierce with your eyes the subtle movements. Feel with your body the currents and shift accordingly. You can do it. . . I know you can. . . because you and I are the same. We have primordial forces that belong to all animals. We are beautiful animals that now need to bring this base primal force to the forefront. Remember. . . remember who you are. Recover these latent energies that are now resurfacing. Receive them in love and understanding. Otherwise our anger and our fear, through their depths of fury and fright, will try to corner you. Their purpose . . . that you move into the current, the new terrain. So become the explorer, the adventurer, the seeker and settle no more for the stationary place you are at now. Settle only for the New land.

— · ● · —

**We are dehumanizing our children
in our educational system**

The stress and anxiety of these school children is what breaks apart the pieces in the realm of Heaven. Stress programs away from peace. Instead we need to instill the joy of learning and move away from the competition, the methods and the strivings of keeping up with the Joneses of China, Japan, Europe and other nations. All nations need to recall and align their beat to the rhythm upon the earth portion that they walk and lay. This land, known as the Land of the Turtle that now moves into the Land of the Hare, needs to do the same – walk to the pace of the earth underneath our feet, and that is the rhythm of individual attention and pace – of individual liberty and freedom, that is of joy, playfulness, and an open playground in the realm of discovery, imagination, and creativity. Now is the time to revert to when we employed less time constriction and less rush among our children, so as they developed the creative, entrepreneurial minds they have become today. So let's take from the past and combine this with the virtue, integrity, and spiritual learnings of today so that we can develop an even more precise, more caring and attentive ideal for each individual child. The arts, music, movement, nature, playtime, and exploration are fundamental in the spirit of our children, of who we are – of where we are going and the future we want and the future that is being given to us!

Open the door, acknowledge, accept, learn and balance.

———·●·———

It is quite absurd to conceive the notion and accept the belief that our educational system will flourish and prosper when grades are the indicating factor of success; test scores dictate the movement of moneys to schools; faster, quicker, and more material are thrown to the students in the misconceived hope, erroneous expectations, and mistaken belief that we are producing a country ready to succeed in the future. To this I say: May our successes be in love, joy, and peace. All other successes are an illusion of the distorted mind.

———·●·———

At each level of vibration, things are perceived or seen differently. It is a matter of simply being so by nature. One example we can say, is that water is water at one vibration, ice at another, and vapor at another vibration. By nature, the laws, the function, use and expression of water at each vibration is unique and different. Simply put, water under certain conditions will turn into ice or vapor. Same with our earthly vibrations, under certain conditions the vibration in our body can change and adjust to the outside and inside force/conditions/laws. You can say we are a product of our vibration.

There are two sets of time:
nature's time and man's mind time.
It is important to work within both realms of time.
It seems to me that most of us lean towards working only
with man's mind time.

———•—

We need to embark on the studies and
enlightenment of spiritual intelligence.

———•—

The idea, the trick, is that we adults must adapt to the incoming souls – the children among us. Not the other way around, that children must adapt to the world that adults have created.

In particular to schooling, we adults must adapt our teaching ways to the new abilities and the ways of the children, which is quite different than what we currently have in place. These changes need to be done quickly, as if continued, they can have long-term disturbing effects on the children.

———•—

The pearls of life are indeed a task.

Now is the moment within our life studies where we can no longer listen just to our Heavenly Father, nor just to our Earthly Mother. We need to bring both into the picture and unite them with their counterpart. Heavenly Father unites with Earthly Mother to give us the understanding, the capabilities, the knowledge of Heaven placed on Earth.

———·•·———

Life is but a school of learning. Learn!

———·•·———

To every truth there is a distortion.
To every lie there is a truth.
One is pleased and content, accepting of the moment's truth within the distortion and understanding.

———·•·———

We have been fighting all along over the words written in our books.

There are different levels to your soul—
Different consciousness to your soul.

———·•·———

Yes
No
Maybe so.

I don't know.

———·•·———

There is a purpose and a place for everything.

———·•·———

There are different levels of understanding
and different levels of experience
and different levels of life.

———·•·———

We are the fallen angels. We are rising back up.

In any relationship, you want to nourish it with proper action and words.

———·●·———

Certainty of anything is unfolding to reveal there is not much certainty in anything we perceive.

———·●·———

We know nothing much and all we can do is bask in the bliss of God. As soon as one enlightened curtain opens, another is behind it.

———·●·———

Be void of the annoying Selves
that
   have
      attached to your liking.

<u>Keep the Same Patterns</u>

Keep thinking the same thoughts,
saying the same words,
doing the same actions,
and the patterns will repeat themselves and the
results will stay the same.

Extend your thoughts,
change your words,
change your actions,
and you create new patterns
and the results will change.

———•●•———

*We must become each a grinding force
and we must fly the new winds like geese –
each taking turns leading.*

Ask your healing Father and Mother
to purify your thoughts, words and actions.

———•●•———

Deliver us from the creations of assumed joys that
deliver triumphantly and temporarily

———•●•———

Accept conflict with the notion to sit at the table of love to
resolve it, so the conflict can be presented, nurtured,
inspected and resolved.

———•●•———

We must listen to the heart,
but never leave out reason.
We must always bring in reason,
but never leave out the guidance of the heart.
Tie them together within your Kingdom
and you will reign in peace.

Become conscious of your soul –
Then become a conscious soul.

— ·•· —

Everything is set within the darkness.
Everything stems within the light.

— ·•· —

All is done in the name of love.
The question is what degree of love.

— ·•· —

In a war each fights for love.

— ·•· —

Every move up in vibration
dissolves the truth below it.

What we do to others
opens the doors to be done to us.

———·•·———

Just because "it" solves the problem
does not mean the medicine is appropriate.

———·•·———

If I could change anything from my past, I would
be negating an experience lived, the lesson given,
the learning taught, the path given.

———·•·———

You are who you are
because the universe is what it is,
and the universe is what it is
because you are who you are.

All words have connection to an emotion. Words are alive – thus I want to use them correctly because I understand God's magic in them to create.

———·●·———

Never override your power. Not even my words are absolute over your disposition and your Being.

———·●·———

They who walk the spiritual path will be challenged at each gate of Heaven. You must prove yourself ready upon the doors that shall open. It would be an error in love to let someone in who is not ready for the task.

———·●·———

Your first and foremost job is of the heart.
Align the heart within – so as to
shower the heart without.

Act the way you imagine
and believe yourself to be.

———•—•———

REMEMBERING

The issue is to remember –
on one end it is what we remember and hang onto,
on the other end is what we have forgotten and need to
remember.

———•—•———

Today and always remember
who you are

———•—•———

Words can persuade,
but actions dictate.

You can say 'I love you' till you're blue in the face.
Align those words with proper action.

Take the Breath, expand it in saying these words
and properly activate the body to express the love
spoken.

———·●·——

The instant of the moment caught
in the blink of an eye –
can change the world within
and the world outside.

———·●·——

The ego needs love. It needs attention.
It's okay. Sometimes it's in the stage of an infant,
or a small child. It wants the world to notice it
and to take care of its every need.
Once in a while, that's okay.

To be clear: we are more magnificent
than we can possibly imagine and know.

———•———

On one level, we have decoded the pattern, we have
solved the riddle, and some of us don't know it yet.

———•———

There is a Mother aspect that is nurturing to a point of
suffocation.

Like everything else, it has its purpose.

———•———

What is darkness to one is light to another.

Revelation: We would perish without darkness –
all light would consume us.

———•—

The tendency to believe in drama as substance for the soul,
assures us we stay connected to the illusion of self
importance, and the forgotten chance of unyielding power.

———•—

We are independent of our talents.
We are not our talents.
We are independent of our personality.
We are not our personality.

———•—

A way of life is not taught.

It is learned by trial and error.

Every moment has been made perfect. Within the past lies the opportunity to correct in the present.

———·●·———

Even the needle in the haystack is within perfection.

———·●·———

It seems we literally tear ourselves up when we do not like ourselves. The emotional hatred towards one's self becomes alive, and one can feel the presence of this Being.

———·●·———

THERE ARE SO MANY TRUTHS that are accurate at a certain level, but would be inaccurate at another level. The tricky part is insisting that your experienced truth and mental conclusion applies to everyone else when they are at a totally different level of Being (configuration of light). All their combinations of bodies (physical, mental, emotional, spiritual and more) depict just as much an accurate truth at their level as your truth at your level.

As we grow or expand in conscious of the upper levels, keep the awareness of the lower levels.

———·●·———

There is a higher truth
that negates what is a truth right now.

———·●·———

These times are about finding our strength.

———·●·———

I can tell you everything is in perfection

... for the learning

Everything is so clear and in place ...

for now...

— ·•· —

IN RELATIONSHIPS, MANY THINGS CAN OCCUR that can be seen as pitfalls. Especially as we move into higher workings of sexual energy with our partner/love/dating relationships. It is still my experienced belief that to walk carefully around these pitfalls at optimum levels, for both adults and teens, it is ideal to ferment the relationship and delay the sexual activity until the subtle cement and glue of the relationship has had time to be applied, settled, and dried.

— ·•· —

Most of us can condemn another's action without being in that time or place, or simply stated, we say that we would or would not do something that someone else did if we were under those same circumstances. Yet, when we are placed under those circumstances, our mind shifts to a personal experience. And what we once spoke of suddenly does not apply to our own experience of the moment in the flesh.

This is why it is futile to condemn another.

How and when do you reach beyond
the comfort of your knowing?
>When do you expand your mental and emotional
>limits and boundaries?
And how and when do you walk further from your
current physical outline and capabilities?

It is a fine line indeed.
>Bring in the Holy Trio in communion,
>in Marriage,
to keep you focused on the thread of balanced
centeredness within the scope of all the possibilities.

—·●·—

It is a fine line to walk between settling within your
capabilities and abilities, or walking through the Ring of
Fire.

—·●·—

CONCEPT: many souls were "forced/sent" here to earth
at this time against their likening for the higher learning
opportunity.

Many folks for this reason may feel as if they don't want to
be here, are out of place and don't belong on Earth. A bit
different than feeling you don't fit in with the crowd or
peer group. It extends beyond that.

NON-ACCEPTING *of our past prevents us from accepting why we are the way we are and who we are. It devoids us of the fact that we are all on a path of discovery and of evolution. In accepting the past, we then can prepare for the present with all the ingredients of resilience, understanding and compassion. If we fault the past we continue to fault the present. It is in the understanding that we can accept, and it is in the accepting that we transform and untangle the energy cord; from this understanding and knowing we build a solid future.*

———·•·———

Keep Vigilant. We keep vigilant by avoiding getting tangled up in the emotional drama of the material life. Focus on the stream, on the flow of light - without throwing oneself into the script. Instead become the observer.

BLOCKAGES OCCUR WHEN you do not allow an experience to be with full acceptance, with the understanding that it is in itself in perfection, flowing and in movement with His hand. There is nothing that can be out of sync, yet there is the inability to comprehend or imagine the possibility of perfection within each moment, within each breath breathed by each of you. This cannot be understood because we believe that in difficult times the omnipresence of God is not there. We have forgotten He is there, He is here, He is everywhere every instant of every moment. We have forgotten and in the forgetting it is a moment in time, in perfection of how it is to be. The class course is almost complete and He will come to sweep away the veils – the curtains so that we may progress towards the next act of the play of resolution.

———•—

The error is in applying at this earthly level
certain freedoms and ways
of the higher levels.

Empty your cup –
by allowing the truth to shed its skin.

———•—•·———

For me, an enlightened individual is he who is aware and has understanding of the works of Below and Above and is aware that he is but a child still between the crib and his playpen. So he savors and wonders in awe at the world around him continuously discovering with joy the embrace of God.

———•—•·———

WHAT IF EMOTIONS ARE REAL? In other words, alive. What if an emotion is an intelligent Being with needs, wants and thoughts, and experiences emotions itself?

If this is so, how is it decided how they influence us, and do we influence it – the emotion?

My understanding, my experience is yes, emotions are alive and they need to find expression of themselves too, just like we seek to express ourselves. And my experience and knowledge is yes, they do teach/influence us and likewise we can teach/influence that emotion.

WHAT IS IT THAT WE ARE TIED TO? What is it that bears the marks of heavy chains, restless nights, angry pouting, discord and a frown upon your forehead?

It's the buying into the game. You know – buy low, sell high. Do unto others only to benefit oneself.

We use our intuitive, intelligent abilities to connect the dots at lightening speed as an incentive to gain upon the other. Sometimes we do it as an innocent game. Sometimes we are very calculating and determined to be at the top no matter the cut we place among our brothers.

The child is not yet aware, that cutting and deleting another is a mistaken and temporary fill to the emotions, and that in the cutting, he cuts himself. He still needs to realize that the actions that extend and expand his playmate, is the longer lasting emotion that fills a purpose and extends and provides true growth and power over one's self.

———•—

Remember, there are many realms within this realm, each with its set of laws.

Notice your Higher Self – another part of you. Activate it by letting it observe you! Let it observe your thoughts, your words, your feelings and emotions, your actions, and observe the speed of time between the movement of all this and the mind. Break down the thought or what you see – perceive and keep track of the message relay system of the mind. Love and discover how it functions and how you can take the control in your hands and change the channels with the guidance of your Higher Self to what is best for you.

———•———

He who demeans and enslaves a woman so she stays in her place according to religious law; who fights a brother because he is of a different religion, race, ethnic group, sect, or from a different land; who uses punishment, sin and hell as attributes of God; who discredits another based on sexual preference; who enslaves another through the concepts and credibility to the belief of a righteous God – is in the need of an earnest awakening to Life and all the splendors and truth it offers.

I need not reinvent the wheel – every medicine for your soul, your mind, your body, your emotions is already at your reach. Ask – seek and the Medicine will come to you. Awaken your ears and listen, awaken your mind and observe, awaken your eyes and see, awaken your smell and smell, awaken your taste and taste, so when the medicine arrives, you will know it has arrived.

———·●·——

There is nothing that is out of place —
All is within the realm of perfection.
Every step, every move, every action
provides the goal towards eternity.

———·●·——

I have noticed it is time to change our planet's dream.
We need to move away from the adrenaline necessities of the
spells of emotional drama. Instead, let's get hooked on the
content glory of solid, joyful, grounded peace.

———·●·——

WHAT IF ... what occurred yesterday and what occurs today is to ensure the bright occurrences of tomorrow? In other words – the moves of yesterday's history are ensuring the progress of tomorrow.

The task at hand is to reconcile
Good/Bad, Birth/Death, and God/Evil.

This reconciliation marks the end of duality
as viewed from our current assigned learning pad
and our current experiencing.

In reconciling God / Evil we embrace God, and we reconcile the past and the present. We establish a foundation, establish faith and seal understanding.

In reconciling Birth / Death we affirm Life. We then comprehend and are of the knowledge that we have everlasting Life and are immortal.

In reconciling Good / Bad we reconcile the first step of duality and we stand in the calm of the eye of the hurricane and good/bad becomes more of an opinion or preference than a judgment or an attachment. We resolve judgment, sin, and innocence.

Money consciousness is no exception
to the evolving nature of mankind's world.

———•—•———

At the bottom of every move and action is money.
At the top of every move and action is God.

Do not doubt that the world turns without either of these
magnificent forces.

One of God, one of the children of God.

———•—•———

Money makes the world go around...
And so does gravity.

— James Lunga, age 13

———•—•———

I am constantly revising what I know!

THE ANSWER IS PEACE – PIECE BY PIECE

On a
Mental Note

Occasionally, mentally deranged,
But otherwise I am fine.

— ·•· —

It's not so much what happens or occurs –
but how one mentally digests the outside occurrences
within oneself.

— ·•· —

*We all know about emotional support,
now let's talk of mental support.*

— ·•· —

*I am the dedicated and inspired traveler in the
journey of the mind.*

Observe your thoughts without judgment, without
getting hooked. Let them come and go and just
watch them, with everlasting joy.

———•●•———

Just because you know –
    does not mean you understand.

———•●•———

There is such a thing as living it and experiencing it
through the Mind or through the Heart as there is living it
and experiencing it in the flesh.

———•●•———

Mental illness: perhaps, suffice to say right now that none
of us escape this misnomer.

When the mind recognizes itself inside the
Mind of God,

It is mind shattering...

— ·•· —

The mind needs to be busy; otherwise, it will conjure up
all these nasty thoughts in which it delights
in your fearful response.

— ·•· —

I am a scientist of the mind, intrigued with curiosity as to
how your delicious mind works. I want to know how it
beats . . . its tempo to life.

In this, I challenge you to a duel of the mind.

— ·•· —

Mirror, mirror on the wall.
Who's the craziest of them all?

You are, my love! You are!

Thank you.

The mind does not capture miracles as easily as the hardships. That's why the hardships are for the learning.

Most of the time your mind actively dismisses the miracles as non-believable.
The pain awakens the belief.
The point is to get to a steady point of belief,
and no longer need the pain to remind.

So steady the mind and
keep to the knowledge.

Keep planting in the spring, harvesting in the fall, resting in the winter. Remember, so as not to be short on the harvest or the feeding.

———•———

Allow the God Mind to surface.

———•———

Your mind says yes – your body may later say otherwise.

PEACE OF MIND
PEACE OF SOUL

The
Physical Body
&
Death

MY MESSAGE IS:

> The body is not to be left behind as we seek
> higher planes. The body is indeed a temple
> that needs to be our altar for all we do and say.

—·●·—

Say unto yourself –
I am but eternal life.

—·●·—

We can get to a part where we will not need to constantly
replace or repair ourselves at a molecular, mental,
emotional, or physical level.

—·●·—

I know when you die, you just wake up
and it's another day somewhere else.

Now is the time to open the doors and explore the healer in you. Anything is within the possibilities to restore, to heal, to complete. First is the realization that our organs, body parts and various systems are alive. I mean by this, that they have their own independent thoughts, emotions and feelings – apart from the thoughts in your brain or emotions and feelings you experience. So your heart, your liver, your spleen, your hands, your feet, your nervous system, etc., are alive and independent of you, yet within you.

—–•·•–—

The body speaks

—–•·•–—

We will discover that we encompass bacteria, germs, and viruses not only inside our bodies – but that similar Beings also reside outside our body, and live within our aura and among various external unseen parts of us. We will discover that many of theses "Beings" cause a major influence on our mental, emotional and physical body disposition.

What if every tooth in your mouth has a story to tell, an opinion to give, a thought to share, information to pass on, feelings and emotions to talk about?

—·•·—

There is more to physical death than most people realize, contemplate, or are even aware of. In addition, there is more to the continuation of life after the death of the physical body than most folks can come to understand or believe. As such, life in and of itself is eternal.

—·•·—

Father – In peace and joy I approach you, and ask you to open and show me the way towards proper healing.

—·•·—

PRAYER

I do not want to be a burden with fatigue.
Dear Lord, show me the way to mend the thoughts of my emotions so as to have the strongest of mental health and the sturdiest of body.

LIFE IS ETERNAL

You already have it. It has never been taken away from you. It is yours. More than a birthright, it is a majestic living breath placed and crowned upon you with the eternal flame of His love, showered in every place around you for eternal Life. You could not exist right now without the wreath of eternal Life placed upon you. Rejoice as the crown removes the thorns from the emptiness of life – so that you may experience true love, true joy, and true Being. You are eternal in His love. This is His love.

———•———

Envision it as it is now. . .
Healed –
because it is.

———•———

Anorexia is the desperate cry of the soul to feed it.

———•———

Are you so riddled with illness
that the healer within
has lost touch on the healing?

You are a force –
contend with it
and show the world
who you are.

Heal thyself.

— ·•· —

I know health can be restored to the mental,
emotional, spiritual and physical bodies
to full capacity, and in totality.

— ·•· —

PHYSICAL DEATH

The continuation of life is a remarkable thing to witness. It brings peace, joy, and an expansion of the heart and mind of the wonders of God.

Just like we usually have someone assist us when we are born here, there are many ready to assist us when we are born to the next realm.

———·•·———

You have a condition within you that has materialized within the God that you are. If you can bring it on, you can certainly work with it and transform it.

———·•·———

Cancer is the ultimate expression of the war going on inside.

———·•·———

TALK TO THE BODY

You are a beautiful home for my soul and spirit. You are beautiful in every sense and every moment. You function with much beauty, and perfectly.

We encapsulate a whole universe
that is alive within us.

What does this mean - a whole universe
alive within?

It means that every organ and body system is separate
from the total you
in thought, in mind, and in emotions.
It means each part can speak.

And it has a voice. If you listen
it will communicate.

———·●·———

IT IS A STARTLING SHOCK, followed by overwhelming
wonder, to hear liver talk, to feel sadness of the womb, to
feel and discuss anger of hand muscle. You read these
written words but for your world to personally experience
this, is the lesson only you can read with your own words,
touching each page with your own feelings, and
developing a sensation from the story that you want to
share so excitedly with all your discovery . . . the truth. . .
the truth of your world, your Being. So we breathe and
ground ourselves as to not be lost in this New Land. It is
important to know there is nothing to conquer or amass,
but only to experience within the context of who you are.

Our organs and body systems, each have its own chakra system, its own separate emotional body and mind body.

———•———

The physical body's mind can not differentiate between past, present, and future. Its fears of yesterday, and its concerns for tomorrow become immediate.

———•———

THIS IS THE TIME to get to know yourself. You must come to the comprehension that you are not your physical body, but that you do listen to it, communicate with it, work with it, and let it guide you. Understand that you are not your emotions, but that you do work with them as a guiding light along with the mind and the aspects of the heart. We must train our emotions so as to center them and balance them. On one level, you are part of the Mind. With this you work to expand your understanding, your comprehension, your awareness, your consciousness. I hope you dedicate time, effort, energy and money into the study of Who You Are.

PIECE BY PIECE YOU BUILD PEACE WITHIN

Spider Woman
&
Animals

The language of love
is of the animal kingdom.
     The words that come through
     are love portions
     from Snake and Spider potions of love.

Let me just place my scent upon you

- Spider Woman

———•——

At the level of total, immense and all encompassing love what is taken into account is that which cements us all – our complete Being. In Spider Woman's words and dance, she showed me that as the creator and weaver of all – she takes all her brood and holds them in her world of arms and no one is higher or lower by actions, but equal by being her creation.

AN ANIMAL'S DEATH

You would be surprised at the complexities and intricate
work occurring in the other realms in preparation to
receive the birth of an animal
in death transition.

———•●•———

THE ANIMAL KINGDOM

We can use our animal instincts to our advantage on a
conscious level. There is a very close bond and family unit
with the entire animal kingdom. We may be at the top of
the hierarchy on one level, but on other levels they are
equal to us. In fact we are them – and each animal is an
archetype – a blueprint of who we are. They are our
teachers. They are part of our essence and make us who
we are.

———•●•———

Our brothers of the lower Kingdom (animal Kingdom)
always remind us of who we are
and what we are made of.

SPIDER WOMAN SHE

Look at a spider. Know that she is an insect.
But she is more than insect.
She is an archetype.
Know she is more than an archetype. She is a Being,
and she is re-emerging.
She is creator and weaver.
She is the keeper of Knowledge.
She is the creator, carrier and bringer of the written word.
And the word creates.

She is midwife.
She has awakened again as midwife to her children who are
being born again.
She is the bringer of the past,
the now and the future into One.
Breathe in and breathe out
and become One with her.

—•—

The Realm of the Dogs is one of the guardians of the earth.

Animals – Our Younger Brethren

It is our duty, forgotten yet to be recalled, to show them the way of love and of growth. We have to bring to the forefront the Law of Will – free choice – and we gravely violate this law with them, because we have not pierced the veil of Knowledge. It is time to recall, to progress to keeping within the laws of nature. Yet it is not necessary to remember the laws when and if our hearts are open to seeing the way of love and then following that path. For most of us, that door within our hearts has not opened yet, so through knowledge of the mind, let's recapture our power, our dignity and ourselves.

When we use our brethren in testing, in ways of intimidation, of physical pain, of torture, in ways that disregard that they are a part of creation, made by the Creator, in ways that show our naivety and ignorance as to who they are and how their lives play out in the role of time and within the past, present, and future, I can tell you with assurance, we enslave ourselves and the message is clear: we are behind grade in the knowledge of the workings of Life on a spiritual and metaphysical level. Because of this naivety and ignorance, we pay dearly with energies outside of us that take advantage of this ignorance, because they will employ with us what we employ with our younger brethren in disregarding their free will.

Animals from a spider to a horse to a gorilla to a snake to an octopus to a dinosaur, all experience emotions, have feelings and thoughts and experience anger, fear, depression, love, joy, and so forth. They have intricate lives as we think not possible.

I feel that during our current times, where Mother Earth energies are vibrant, strong and demanding, that it is in our best interest to work with our animal totems or at least relate and connect at some level with animals. It is Her request and calling that each of us connect on a deeper level with the rest of the animal kingdom. It is time to recognize their power beyond the seen, their abilities and nature beyond the physical world and the teachings and knowledge they bring.

———•◦•———

For all of those that have a hand in neutering specifically dogs and cats, it is recommended to delay the neuter until six months. There is a rush to neuter or spay early – to offset the chance or possibility of creating more creatures. However, more intense is the weight of removing the essential, internal communication channels from these Beings at a premature rate. In the hopes and thought of doing what is in their best interest, based on our feelings and perceptions, we cloud a necessity and basic right intended by natural cause to be in order. More of a balance is to allow these creatures, mostly from shelters and pounds, to obtain their needed structure and then remove their reproductive systems preferably no earlier than six months of age. In this way, we employ a balance between nature's time and man's time.

I Am All and Everything

The spirit that rises, the tomorrow that brings,
the curiosity that awakens and leads the spark to its place.
I have come to bring the flowers of love
to my ancestors in peace. I have come to show my children
her place - I have come to bring the steps to the future life
among the people of earth,
so that I can rest in my kingdom above.

———•———

*I am a lover in love with the loving
And this love is my initiation.*

PIECE BY PIECE,
THREAD BY THREAD,
WE WEAVE THE WEB OF PEACE
AROUND THE WORLD

Randomness

Who am I?
Who am I?

If you take away my emotions, who am I?
If you take away my thoughts, who am I?
If you take away my mind, what am I?

Without emotions,
do I exist?
Without thought,
do I exist?

— · ● · —

HEAVENLY LOVE – is without alignment to a cause, action, or state of Being. It simply is an expression, a very thorough, deep, filtrating energy of complete, perfect, disinterested love for the individual.

Its concept is similar to the love felt for a newborn, for an infant. Add a more complete systematic, radiating love component to every cell and you have Heavenly love.

Improve yourself – improve human kind.

—•—

Go to the limits of your longing.

—•—

Why on earth do we walk,
    determined to become,
        nothing more than a
            conglomerate Being
                of magnified emotions?

—•—

Stop the massacre of who you are!
    Stop the war you ignite in
    contradiction of who you are.

We speak the same language
We are just fighting over words.

One thing is to think it – and say it –
another thing is to live it.

———·•·——

Do not wait for someone else to change the world.
Start
The change with
You!

———·•·——

I am a mystic that demystifies.

———·•·——

Ah, the void.
The busiest place in the World,
Where everything is set and happens.

I entice you to find your voice, to
develop your individuality, to

move from
psychic ability to
spiritual insight

as we work with esoteric
and metaphysical tools of knowledge and understanding
to elevate who you truly are.

The improbable is within reach
as you open to divine wisdom and
experience it directly without becoming lost in it.

———·●·———

Where to begin of my story ...?
Where to start of all the beginnings of starts?
Of the beginning of paths?

I would not know where to commence!

———·●·———

You are valuable.
Don't let anyone make you believe differently.

WHEN IT IS TIME TO WAKE UP –

Life will come and find you
and wake you up.
It's a given!

—–·•·—–

I am everything
and the nothingness
and the emptiness in-between.

—–·•·—–

Life is hard!
Take a laxative.

If we are all actors in the stage of life –
who wrote the script?

———·●·———

Pain is a beautiful catalyst
from which vast pristine volcanic laden soil can
become rich and fertile lands.

———·●·———

Life is a balance between what I feel
and what I know.

———·●·———

I've melted down these essences and bore a child

I am very serious in my living, as
living is a serious business.

———·•·———

Even the bitter has its medicine to give.

———·•·———

We are like the trees –
Sometimes giving our life to the woodcutter so that
the carpenter can use our trunks and limbs
for the necessities of life.

———·•·———

Live and remember.

The King said, "Let there be light!"
The Queen said, "There is already light."
He said, "But you have not seen my brilliance."
She said, "Ah – but you have not seen *my*
brilliance!"

———·●·———

What we are going to do
is acknowledge the forces and
love the force that we are.

———·●·———

In the face of everything Life has to offer,
it helps to be resilient.

———·●·———

I am a small voice in this plentiful sea.
A voice that speaks her truth.

And that encompasses everything.
My notion of love is pure.
It's finding the portion
Within the motion
That gets exhilarating at times.

———•—

You have to experience to become something else.

———•———

I am but one river in the endless
mountain of time
The stream shoots forth in spurts
It settles in pools and lakes
I am but peace upon the calm waters
I am the rising turbulence beneath the waves
Settle me, settle me — and I will sleep

I am strong. I am powerful. I am wicked.

— ·•· —

In spite of the heaviness that I see
and the darkness that I feel,
        come my brother,
            I know we will figure this out.

— ·•· —

If God is everywhere, why beat Him up with the disguise
of evil?

— ·•· —

How do I put into words
what is most sacred in thought?
How do I spell out what meaning has not?
How to print streams of consciousness
with no answers, with no particular way?

Better to be a half asleep obedient child
than a fully awake disobedient child.

——·●·——

So prevalent is the desire to be more
than what we are.

——·●·——

I am no less, upon the tears shed
        and thus the weeds of time grow
            upon my reflected face.

I am no more no less the time invested upon the
        planted garden of the moving
            parts of soul's time –

yet inquire –
and hear the rays of sunshine reflect their hour
upon the mattress of my soul where I lay.

I am no more than more and no less than less –
        for eternity is the eternity of my moment,
            of my hour, and reflected
                in my eternities of time.

| make music.
| play the strings of the piano of life and
| connect, in harmony and melody, the moment.

———·●·———

I am a poet to my own music
I am the rhythm to my beat

———·●·———

I a rose alright!
"I thought you were a sunflower?"
"I arose the sunflower within me."

———·●·———

FAITH

In knowing, I sit in the throne at the center of Being.
Nor swayed by the right
nor swayed by the left.
I hear my two partners in equal disposition.
My love intertwines them in the love canal up through the
spiral, resting, breathing, leaning here and there. Restored
once again in the pull up and released, tighten and release;
it's a swaying up and down, right and left. My true love
surrounds me on all four – I am a child of all corners and
my breath anchors me down. As I can play away to the
realm of surround ecstasy – easy up easy down and
around.

The ice is melting and you can take off your coat.
Spring is here. Go ahead and thaw out.

— . ● . —

Resist, Thaw and Become

— . ● . —

At this point,
I have decidedly decided to live life!

— . ● . —

With incredible joy and love for humanity, we can
put forth our depth of pain, sadness, fear, and
despair, into the bowl of humanity's consciousness,
so that another may dip into our hardships and
effort and gain from it.

— . ● . —

There is more to all this than there is to all that.

I know all that **I know** is not all that **I know**.

———.•.———

There are times when nothing matters –
Because all is in its right place.
Nothing out of place.

———.•.———

I do want to see! It's just the little kid in me.

———.•.———

There are many facets to the diamonds of my soul.

———.•.———

There is so much I don't know
compared to what I know.

I am a painter with words –
Scattered canvases here and there –
Tattered words left undone –
Music painted with imaginary lines –
Movement with erasable, traceable scribbles in this
forehead of mine.
Nothing empty sits except an easel here and there-
Brushes come and go –
And everything else is
Life with a flair

———·●·———

I will take a chance that life will throw me
the chance of my life.
            And so I will not tiptoe through the night
                    but I will dance the night away.

———·●·———

I spoke to the moths in the pantry this morning –
"I know you have your place and a purpose,
but can you find a different place and a different
purpose?"

There are diamonds to be seen in the chaos of living.

———•●•———

I bring forth the joys of my world to yours.

———•●•———

Predict what to do today
For the needs of tomorrow.

———•●•———

I REALIZE I DO NOT KNOW *much or exactly what is going on, yet I put myself gently and easily in God's hands and I am in peace.*

———•●•———

It's not so much what happens to us –
but how we react to what happens to us.

This overcoming influx of joy becomes me
and I have no other choice but to be in Heaven. . . . .
    But I have dishes to wash,
    beds to make and bills to pay. . . .
    So I bring Heaven down to me and the dishes are
done, the bed is made, and the bills are paid – while I live
on earth and Heaven directs me.

———·●·———

We are children of the realm and
the universe embraces us
and rocks us lullaby in her arms.

    Gently sleep my little one
    and wake to know that
    life wonders in your arms.

———·●·———

Arise my child and become the rose that you are
and bring your bouquet of flowers to Her –
The Great Mother –
Who understands the child.
She is the greatest lover –
Because She knows the way –
And Her way is His way –
He who stands at the right hand of the Father,
who knows the child,
who is the child,
and leads towards the resolution of mistakes.

She is the face of eternity,
He is the realm of Love.

She is the Queen of eternity,
He is the King of the house.

She is the Queen of justice,
He is the King of Love.

She dictates where,
He shows how.

Together their love abounds
In distinct order of things.
They manage to come around
And unite their shortcomings,
He with Hers, and she with his.

Phantom not He reigns and rules,
Within the order of Her house.

She sweeps beneath the order
And takes with Her what is Hers
And we have already settled, Hers is
Eternity – so march accordingly.
Pave the way – for as She comes –
So does Eternity

I am calling to lend my support to you as a human being, in the knowing that you are no different than I am.

———·●·——

I am who I am.
How can I be any different,
other than to be the I am I am.

———·●·——

Life itself is an abyss
with eternal fountains
from which we drink.

———·●·——

Dance is the match that ignites the fire in my soul.

— Yadira Rodriguez, age 14

———·●·——

You have to give time its time.

Hay que darle tiempo al tiempo.

— Colombian Proverb

Father,

I have let go of fear towards life because I know you are with me. With total trust, I take hold of your hand and I walk through the world with complete confidence.

Thank you father, that it is so.

Padre,

He soltado el miedo a la vida porque sé que tú estás conmigo. Confiadamente, me cojo de tu mano y voy por el mundo en completa seguridad.

Gracias Padre, que es así.

—Dr. Arturo Estrada

———•●•———

The bad is simply the good misunderstood and furthermore incorrectly applied.

El mal es simplemente el bien mal entendido y peormente aplicado.

—Dr. Arturo Estrada

YES – BRING ME PEACE,
MEAL BY MEAL, SLICE BY SLICE

His Peace

It is His battle, our journey, your path.

———•—•—•———

Jesus saw the unification process in himself and thus accomplished the uniting and the tying of the two within – male/female, positive/negative, heaven/earth.

———•—•—•———

Begin with me, my breath, and storms will cease.

———•—•—•———

Jesus in all sense was a man - just like the man of today, with all the desires, restraints, weaknesses, and struggles we all encounter.

———•—•—•———

**May the strength that you seek -
Be of His.**

You are everything.
You are the void,
you are eternity and every step in-between.
You are the joy of the sorrows,
you are the fountains of youth,
of spring, of old, of new.

You are nothing that isn't.
You are all that is.
Nothing escapes you,
nothing enters you –
nothing you see is not you –
because you become what you are and you are all.

Rest aside and know you climb to new heights
as a flower reaches to higher sky.
I am with you in eternity and always.

Bear with my words,
bear with the steps aligned for you.
Bear with my knowledge and the doors to
my home are open to you.

———•———

Do not doubt that He indeed looks upon every instant
and makes the instant the way.

I too, have walked the path of the Dark Night of the Soul. A different path than yours. It is filled with emotional upheavals and struggles. It is arduous, hard work, a bumpy road, different bridges to pass, surmountable rivers to cross. But it can lend you the strength to walk alongside Him, to develop perseverance and it is an opportunity to transform your Being to the likeness of His love.

—·•·—

The gift of love is everlasting love.
There is no other gift
worth running for or from.

—·•·—

I AM THE PRESENT. I am the past and the future to come. Believe in my resurrection as I will resurrect among you. To each I will bring the tokens of love and pass on the spirit release given unto you. It is my destiny to believe in you as you believe in my destiny. Bring me the joys of deliverance from misconstrued notions and knowledge, and present the ever present self, true self, and true words.

I am beautiful
I am in balance
I am a child of God
I am His reflection of His beauty
I am a reflection of His love
I am His reflection of His perfection

And I have been beside Him, always.
I am His reflection –
And my spark has been and will be of Him always.
I am His gold, His silver, His jewels and diamond,
His spirit and joy.
He walks always with me,
I walk always with Him.

He creates all and since I am with Him,
In Him, Of Him, I create alongside Him.
Understanding this I understand I create all with Him.
The entire universe of God has my paint brush strokes.
And I joyfully accept every artist stroke I paint on
our canvas.

With my words I dance in my studio.
With my thoughts I bring in the colors.
With my actions, I weave the brush upon the canvas.
With my lips I sign my art and there are God's thoughts,
words and actions along side my painting,
together as always, expanding, developing,
the Masterpiece.

And I so gently sit me down in my studio of life that God
and I have built,
and I look at the scenes we have painted.
We look at all the acts acted out.

We marvel at the detail of our brush strokes, the art
created by God, me and all my brothers has infinite marvel
and suspense, infinite direction and strands of storylines,
all nicely assembled in perfect flawlessness.

And in review of one strand of written art
upon the history books of one place, my studio,
I see the strokes we created with my own hand in the
history of our time, our place, our canvas.
The colors of thought used, the words we danced, the
actions we stroked created our history.
I had equal artist participation and time in history, and as
such I have upon reflection on this truth,
made complete what was incomplete.

> Here is my and God's history,
> And so the jury so far is close to balanced
> on the scale.
> The last detail numbers will be weighed,
> and have no doubt that practice makes perfect,
> and each page book will be accepted as perfect.

—·•·—

The greatest love story ever written –
is that you love Him so much
that you went in to find Him.

I've plunged the depths of life and rivered the streams of hell. Oh joy, what a ride to everlasting peace, knowing all is with Him.

———·●·———

I am all the teachings
I am all the breaths
I dispense them all
So that each breath can be a breath
So that each teaching can be taught

———·●·———

I am that light,
I am that energy that has travelled
through many worlds.

———·●·———

I am aware and knowing of the nakedness of my mind, thoughts and actions – whether I show Him my true colors or whether I hide them from Him and from myself.

Opening every bit of me from eons of thoughts and words to actions that compose who I am.

— ·●· —

I am the storm. I cause the storm.

— ·●· —

Father, I am without understanding in this matter.
Father, what is your guidance in this matter?
Father, please give me understanding.

— ·●· —

No matter where I go, He is there.

— ·●· —

Today I will breathe with the total knowing
that I am one with consciousness.
That every breath is in union with Him and every move I
make is to the beat of my heart.

$\mathcal{L}$et His hand

> gently move you to fertile grounds,
> where life flourishes beyond your dreams,
> expectations or desires.

———•———

You will accept the gift of God because you
know it to be true. Search for me in your
depths and I will arise.

———•———

If only words
could depict the messages held in my hand,
my heart would melt in the joy
of the Son and His Father.

———•———

May love touch you deeply,

May wisdom enter your heart,

May joy reach your mind,

And may my peace sway you gently through life.

HIS IS THE PERFECT
MASTERPIECE TO PEACE

The
New World

The world will change completely and thank God it is so. Nothing will be left unchanged.

—·●·—

We march to a new order of harmony - or have you not noticed - that many believe there is disorder and little joy in the present order of things. And so yes, we march pulling with all our might and strength as we drag in the change. The order in the areas of: law, economics, school, legal system, our profession, philosophy, physics, religion, metaphysics, animal kingdom, archetypes, sports, cooking, eating, entertainment, death, living, breathing, sexuality, celebrating, crying, rejoicing, rules, regulations, guidelines, our work, socializing, meditating, yoga, prayer. . . will change. What is really occurring is a necessary and optimum alignment.

—·●·—

These are beautiful times, as we experience the contractions of a birth to a new grade of consciousness.

—·●·—

Prepare yourself for who we are destined to become.

We are on a course and all is well. You may think the world is falling apart and collapsing and you yourself may feel an emotional pull and tug and a sense of an interior collapse. Yet, we are on course for our current evolutionary development. What needs to dismantle will dismantle, what needs to collapse will collapse, yet we ourselves need not dismantle or collapse on a mental or emotional level. If we have the knowledge of what is going on and what to expect to a certain degree, we can remain calm and at peace with the flowering changes upon us. It is frightening because we do not understand or want to understand what is going on nor do we really want to give up so many things to move onto the next level of our Being.

———•●•———

It will be a physical slow down in tempo and speed of the spoken word as we will find the need and comfort in speaking less. What a relief! Extra sound and vision stimuli is no longer warranted. Not only will we be reunited to our inner Being, but we will also reunite with our other earthly and celestial Beings, both of a mass similar to ours and those of mass lighter than ours. It is like a very large family reunion where distant cousins, uncles and aunts, nieces and nephews, fairytales, myths, giants and guardians are welcomed, and where religion swallows its own words and arrives in truth.

There is more to life than what we currently remember, perceive, understand, believe, acknowledge – and more to life's certainties than the current main stream of scientific, mathematical, geological and anthropological understandings.

———•—

The future will consist of more of us
who are in sync with our words,
thoughts and emotions.

———•—

ENORMOUS CHANGE is upon us, world changes that are in alignment, expected and scheduled. These changes cover all arenas – not just one area-not only social, cultural changes and not only individual changes. Some things we will wish will move slower – others we will wish would move faster.

———•—

The New World is a family reunion of myths, religions, stories, truths, accounts, and history.

The concept of not being complete
Of not having enough –
Of all not being in order at the moment –
Will cease.

———·•·———

We are at a period where we need to neutralize the pull
and tug of memories, events and experiences, and where
we need to sit in the balance.

———·•·———

The world will change.
Its fruit is ripe.
Follow the lead of your true heart
and the forest will be clear.

———·•·———

𝒩ature will help immensely
with our movement forward.

$\mathcal{M}$yth and $\mathcal{A}$rchetypes will be transcended

———·●·——

THE TWO REALMS THAT STARTED this new movement into The New World – the streams of communication and sexual energy – will continue to unfold and will bring higher, more spiritual and mature concepts of development.

———·●·——

Know you are safe.
Embrace yourself and get ready for the ride.

———·●·——

In the same way that puberty indicates a change of nature for a child, the nature of many things within humanity have changed and will continue to change.

It really is in its essence no different than adolescence and we humanity, are in a growth spurt.

Everything is changing. The old being thrown out, the new brought in.

———·•·———

ESTABLISH PEACE AND MAINTAIN centeredness and calm during the whirlwind of growth and changes you are encountering.

———·•·———

There is a natural force, a natural drive within nature that forces us to translate our experiences and transform them to a higher level. This is why we will not escape the push to grow and move upwards in mobility towards the natural flow of the birth channel towards our delivery, our birth – so as the saying – as He has promised.

———·•·———

IN ADOLESCENCE, SEXUALITY AWAKENS and the cognitive skills to comprehend the world expand. Likewise, as we move through adolescence in our stage of humanity, our cognitive skills will expand, allowing us to understand ourselves, our path, our world, our place in the world, and the universe at a whole new level. Our understanding of sexual energy will also awaken to new levels of knowledge and understanding. Part of these higher cognitive skills we are developing will clarify and bring a deeper and further understanding of God.

The emotions, new thoughts and
events of tomorrow, may make my
words and promises of today invalid.

Unnecessary to keep them and free to
move within the new confines of
what tomorrow brings.

———.•.——

L ook inside and tell me who you are.
If you do not know –
There are New Lands to be had.

———.•.——

The tree is being transplanted.
The soil is no longer fertile on these grounds.

———.•.——

The greatest leaps and bounds will be in the religious,
scientific, and economic sectors, and within
all aspects of the law.

Enjoy the process, the growth.

Someday, way in the future of time,
you'll retrace these memories and paths in your heart's
soul – and the beauty, the struggle, the joy of this
"adolescent period" will be imprinted in your memory
soul with fondness.

—·●·—

All levels of science, understandings, and spiritual realms
of our Being will be undone so as to bring in the New
Joyous World.

—·●·—

THE ESOTERIC AND THE METAPHYSICAL will leap in
thought, belief, and understanding and new metaphysical
and esoteric worlds will emerge.

—·●·—

It is a new age of spirituality.
One of completeness.
One of totality and beauty.
One of new ways and a higher order.

WE WILL MOVE ON FROM all types of animal slavery. Obsolete will be the bullfights, cockfights, dogfights, animal testing, neutering pets too early, returning animals to the wildlife that prefer to stay within human contact. The New World human will have developed the understanding and the cognitive skills to comprehend the level of complexity and span of intelligence and emotional depth of animals. And most notably, the New Human will have the capacity to communicate thought, feelings, and emotional language with our younger brethren.

———•●•———

TOMORROW'S FUTURE

Certain ways will change quicker than others. Some will be more difficult than others to adjust or to accept. Many others will easily enter, leaving us wondering why we did not promote and accept certain ways of life earlier.

———•●•———

A whole new understanding and a new true meaning of the Bible will arise.

*What we are going to have to face direct in the mirror –
is a new level of truth.*

For example, the teachings of Christ. Suffice to say that we
need to face the current teachings and reflect in the mirror
and accept that there have been incorrect and mistaken
interpretations – a natural process in the life of the child.
Now is the time to review and we are old enough, mature
enough to look at a higher truth.

We have relied on others to interpret the life of Christ and
his teachings for us, when it is each individual's birthright
to tap into the information of this Christ Energy.

———•—•———

We have no choice – we will at some point gleefully join
the movement forward.

———•—•———

*Together we will bring the world to new
standards - that will combine the world's past,
old and new, to newer heights, as mandated by
the Beginning and the End.*

PERCEIVED CONCLUSIONS of the way the body works will be understood at a whole new level. Concepts of food, digestion, chemical reactions, chemical influences and production, beginning and end will elaborate to more extreme perceived notions.

———•———

Our method in ways of sports and competition will march to a higher order and balance.

———•———

LAND MASS CHANGE

Florida will return to the mass lands of the waters – East coast will align its proper service, redirecting the image of the coastline.

Timeframe – I believe in my time, yet search within your hearts, leaving behind the peeled layers of fear – fear of loss, of hard work gone, of memories, of lost habitat or creatures – as this is a never ending cycle. Do not get caught up in the web of loss but in the wonder of things to come.

———•———

ECONOMY – will be turned inside out. Many of the present economic treaties, theories, energy flow, markers, stock market, bonds, treasuries, etc., will cease and/or be turned inside out. And this is good.

Life is a vest of all dialogs, all comforts,
all difficulties, and it is a buffet table of plenty to
choose and savor in the delight of the process of
who we are to become.

— •●• —

The most refreshing future I see is that of change within our laws on all levels.

More and more we are coming to the time and place where rules and boundaries will have to change. The policies enforced, the rules, the laws, the requirements – will be loosened or will be less. Furthermore, each particular incident, circumstance, and/or individual will be independently addressed.

— •●• —

BE GENTLE WITH YOURSELF, as the metaphysical, the esoteric, the healing arts, meditation, yoga, breathing styles, and methods will change too. In addition, the myths and archetypes will have their transformation also. They will be put away and new myths and archetypes of a different style for a new purpose and way, will be brought out. Keep the enthusiasm, love and joy for your studies.

We will no longer be able to expand, grow, rise in studies, economics or stature at the expense of another, at the expense of nature, at the expense of animals. Moving forward, we must contemplate all avenues in our decisions. That includes physical, mental, emotional, and spiritual, and the decision must abide by all these levels.

————•—————

In the New World, we will build understanding at the cellular level. This promotes the ability to see, understand and feel in the skin the precise thoughts and emotions of another. And this, through this manner and way, we build compassion at a deeper level. We build a higher awareness and this leads to an understanding that binds us in an energetic level with others, that we then begin, once again, the molecular structure and process of unification among our species.

Hallelujah!

————•—————

Delight in the changes for they bring you new awareness. Troubled times are past and new beginnings will commence their march. Release the hiccups of your journey by placing trust in your true self.

The New World
brings a new light configuration,
a new drum beat,
a new heart beat for humanity.
It brings higher capabilities and abilities,
knowledge, compassion and balance.

———·•·———

There is a New World among us that sparkles with joy.
Search within the calm heart and the beautiful mind
for the New Lands to discover, navigate, and explore.
Reach for the balance within the Divine Being you are
And let's together create this sparkling New World
Not just for you and me,
But for the souls and children
of today and of tomorrow

———·•·———

Oh, how beautiful the world we are in.
Oh, how marvelous the world to come.

I am of a different beat,
of a different tune.
I say life is not an illusion
and thus God is not an illusion.

Just because there is constant movement and change –
this does not mean the moment in the physical is not real.

It is real! You and I are real.
We are real – in this moment,
and because we are
we can then move to make the changes –
the adjustments necessary to our world,
to our Earth, and to bring the harmony,
the balance, the beauty we so long for.

Join me in this mission.
Join me in a race through time
and be an active work of creation!
Touch the dream within the writings of your heart –
Be the words that flow endlessly
through the pages of your life –
and live the greatest story ever told, because…

with your expressions of true love,
true words, and true actions…

YOU BECOME THE PIECE OF THE PUZZLE THAT JOINS TO CREATE PEACE IN THE WORLD

Martin Luther King

What do you seek?

*We all seek freedom. It truly is not peace, nor love
nor joy, as that is already there. We seek freedom from that
which ties us down and prevents us from being
in love, in joy and in peace.*

*We seek freedom from mental pain, emotional pain,
spiritual pain and physical pain.*

*One man spoke these words
that were written upon time.
These words now are indicative and to be
applied on a level of freedom for the
individual soul and the human spirit.*

*I have a dream
that has been drummed before.
It is a dream of love and joy,
Where God's children
Will sing together –*

*"Free at last
Free at last
Thank God almighty
we are Free at last."*

*And the walls of Jericho,
The chains of slavery,
And the Children of Israel
Will sing a hymn and praise that it is so!*

With Gratitude...

To Life, for her journey.

To Spider Woman, for all that she has shared with me. For her strength, her inspiration and love, her healing force and her love of creation. My heart melts with yours.

With much appreciation to the spectrum of Angels, both Earthly and Heavenly who have entered and added their touch, care, stepping stone, healing energy, dedication, guidance and love to my life. I am with you in love.

To all the teachers and helpers within the various realms of time and space who assisted me throughout various phases of my initiation and who to this day continue to teach and work with me. I treasure your knowledge.

With special thanks to the Native American Indian Guides of the upper realms who set the stage for this incredible journey and who mothered and cared for me as they opened the doors to my initiation. They embrace me to this day with their guidance, love, and wisdom.

With eternal love to my mother, of which words could not describe the depth of love that runs across the bridge of our hearts. Mamita, te quiero[1].

Profound thanks to Dr. Estrada, my spiritual, esoteric, and metaphysical teacher, and mentor. His amazing knowledge and abilities astonish me even more today as I have grown in understanding and in knowledge. Every move and dance between our lives, including life's drop in a bucket chance meeting so fabulously orchestrated, are embraced with much appreciation and love. I admire his tireless and endless effort in

---

[1] **Mamita, te quiero**: Spanish for "Dear mother, I love you."

helping others.

Glowing thanks to Sandy Suminski for her editorial support, keen eye, and exquisite handling of words while keeping to the heartbeat of this book.

Special thanks to Sydney Blauvelt, Mackenzie Blauvelt, Katie Karst, Rob Baker, Katrina Petrovich, Andrew Mize and Teagan Miller for sitting next to me day in and day out helping me with all my computer needs, including typing this manuscript. Your extra pairs of eyes and your input were essential in making this project a reality. Extra kudos to Andrew and Teagan, whose creative suggestions and teamwork added the premium touches to this book.

Warm thanks to all my friends who lent an ear and gave words of encouragement and support when needed...and to Alexis and JoAnna, for reviewing my manuscript and providing their valuable input.

Selected Glossary

Akashic Records – My understanding: A metaphysical library where books with the written stories of all knowledge and every movement of time, light, and space are found for the thoughts, words, energy, and action of each individual on Earth. These written stories can be changed/revised through our effort, time, and energy. These written stories merit contemplation and depth of thought in why they are written in the manner they are written. Look within, about, and around you and contemplate the reason we are so inclined to view riveting and emotionally charged movies and television shows.

Androgynous – Having both male and female physiological and physical characteristics.

Archetype – An original pattern or blueprint of consciousness designed by the Logos to encourage the travel and growth of each individual. This is a living energy that encompasses a programmed field of experience.

Dark Night of the Soul – A stage where Life actively steps in and takes control, and manipulates events to activate necessary emotions, feelings, and thoughts within oneself in order to force one to awaken, grow, and manifest a higher part of oneself. The Oxford Dictionary describes it as a period of spiritual desolation in Christian Theology, suffered by a mystic in which all sense of consolation is removed.

Esoteric – Knowledge or information known to only a select group. My experience has been that the boundaries have been expanded and opened to include a wider audience at this particular time.

Etheric Body – A less dense, subtle vehicle that is integrated into our physical body and provides the transportation of various energies including vitality, strength, vigor, and health to our physical body. It functions on its own without the physical body and it has the exact outline of the physical body. I'll share an interesting story with you. A week or so before the full awakening of my Kundalini energy, I was in a deep sleep and started to wake due to the onset of sudden, severe nerve pain. I slowly opened my eyes and I saw part of my mother's astral arm (recall, she passed on in 1998) pulling my etheric leg — which I could literally see — up toward my head. I laid still and let her do what she needed to do, at the same time being filled with overwhelming joy upon seeing my mother... even if it was just a part of her. My physical body did not move, but just her stretching my etheric leg caused more pain to my physical body. In that moment, amongst the pain, I recognized the astounding nature of what was occurring. After two minutes or so had passed, upon fully awakening, all I could do was communicate to my mother in sign language, "I love you."

Dr. Estrada's description: "Vital body, double etheric, counterpart to the dense physical vehicle of man, animals, and vegetables."

Garden of Eden – The state of unity unaware of the separateness; space/time where the concept of unity is felt and lived but not on a conscious level. Stage of innocence.

God – There are many levels of understanding to this word. On one level it signifies the One creator. For me – the definition at this level is that God is an essence of intelligence, love, and light that exists within and permeates every aspect of time and space with a consciousness that encompasses all and glorifies all. God is not constricted within a Being of some sort, yet God resides within a human Being, a flower, an animal, the sun, the moon, the void, the unseen worlds, all and everything. God is an energy field; a force of pure love that neither denies nor accepts; that has no form and can become any and all forms; that moves beyond comprehension and that stands in complete reign. God is within the stillness and within the roar, within our reach – and beyond our imagination. God is a subtle mist of light, an essence that flows and is within and in between all that is seen and unseen, all that is made, and all that is unmade. Its very essence is love unattached, yet knowing of its full embrace of all that it encompasses. We are part of that mist – that love vibration expressed in more ways than one.

On another level, as children who have forgotten our

true nature, we are yet unaware of the true relationship with the universe and with all the parts that encompass God's creation. As such, we believe and assign to our "Elders" of the universe the word "God." We arrive at this assumption because their capacity, knowledge, and abilities are greater than ours. As we expand in knowledge and cognitive abilities, we will come to recognize and understand that the Elders that we have believed to be the "One" God – are but an expression, much like ourselves, of God.

In fact, these Elders are the very ones that have guided us, known by many names such as Ascended Masters, Spiritual Guides, Prophets, Logos, Saints, Angels, Archangels, Deities, Mohammed, Jesus, Buddha, and other Beings from other planets, dimensions, spheres, our galaxy and other galaxies. They have wanted to bring their knowledge, interpretations, teaching, and guidance to us. As we continue to mature and move through our adolescent stage, with time, and as our cognitive skills widen, we will leap in comprehension at the depth and extension of our world. Then, within our mind's eye the hierarchy of our world – of our space and time – will change, accelerating us to articulate a new, more complete vibration, feel, and expression for the scope of the word "God."

Heaven – Dr. Estrada's definition: "It is Nirvana. There exist seven heavens; in the last two, the saints live in union of Brahma, those that have completed their cycle of existence. In esoteric terms, it is understood as the state of happiness of consciousness that one acquires after passing through purgatory after death. The first, second, and third heaven are situated in the top three regions of the World of Desire. The fourth heaven is located in the region of concrete thought. The fifth is found in the highest region of the World of Thought; in this state, the consciousness of the ego assimilates the fifth essence of all the good realized and materialized on Earth. Up to the fifth heaven, all souls must return by obligation to take on a new physical body. Those of the sixth and seventh heaven take on a physical body if they want to complete a special mission. Nirvana extends to the infinite, and it is not in determined spheres or planes. Those of kind spirit occupy all areas: in space, in the most perfect worlds, and in mansions of the reincarnated. I personally know of Nirvana, and I can assure you that all inhabitants of Nirvana are mighty and omnipotent gods of robust and powerful personality."

202

Inner World – This is the world literally found within the network of our physical, emotional, and mental body. Through our inner world we connect to our outer world, either consciously or unconsciously. This connection reaches out into our solar system, Milky Way, and beyond.

Kundalini – The electrical, metaphysical, spiritual power of the serpent that in the mystical anatomy of tantra and yoga represents the vital, cosmic energy of man. Here is incorporated the true meaning, power and concept of the word "Virgin." It is the female aspect also known as the Virgin Mother – coiled and resting at the base of the spinal column. This female vertical axis energy ascends upward through the Tree of Knowledge in movement and expansion of knowledge.

Light Configuration – Light is a type of communication that encompasses all forms and means. A configuration is a specific blend and combination of the color bands of light, producing a specific vibration. That specific vibration is like a language that relays communication within its specific boundaries, capabilities, abilities, and knowledge of that configuration. There are endless combinations of configurations.

Line of Fire – A narrow path that opens between two walls of fire, purifying emotions. This is the same analogy as the parting of the Red Sea in Exodus – walking the fine path between two walls of water – where water is a universal symbol for our emotions.

Logos – Dr. Estrada's definition: "It is the Word or the second person of the Holy Trinity; in other words the Son, the Christ of the Christian theology. It is the deity or manifested Word; the consciousness that animates all of Life and forms a solar system."

Medicine Woman – In my case, a woman, who through a series of initiations, becomes an intermediary and interpreter between the human and the Spirit world.

Metaphysical – Beyond the physical world; the existence of Life and energy beyond the normal worlds seen by the naked eye.

New World, The – The higher vibrating structure, settings, and programming of our world and our future, paved by the new light configuration already present on Earth. The age of Aquarius. The distinguishing factor between the "old" or previous world and the New World is the change in light configuration. We have entered the New World and it has a higher vibrating light configuration than the "old world." The "end of the world" has already occurred. The old light configuration no longer exists and the New World higher-vibrating light configuration has commenced and it will evolve, mature, and grow into its full splendor of balance and light. At present, we are in the newborn stage of the New World.

Rooms of Books – Metaphysical rooms in a specific space and time where actual, metaphysical informative books are stored for study and review.

Rooms of Knowledge – Metaphysical rooms found in a specific space/time where streams of knowledge are felt, sensed, and understood completely and intensely.

Snake Medicine – The metaphysical, mystical, and spiritual medicine based on the power, knowledge, and electrical force and energy of the serpent. It is a vertical female axis energy and its main purpose is communicator.

Spider Medicine – The metaphysical, mystical, and spiritual medicine based on the power and knowledge of spider energy. It is a horizontal female axis energy and its main purpose is creator.

Spider Woman – Metaphysical Being that encompasses the energy of Creator, Queen, Keeper of Knowledge, of the Written Word, and works with the trilogy of past/present/future.

Underworld – The less physically dense world, yet heavier on an etheric level, located within the Earth.

Bibliography

Cayce, Edgar. Various Readings. A.R.E. Association for Research, Virginia Beach, VA

Myss, Caroline. *Sacred Contracts*. New York: Harmony Books, 2001.

Patterson-Rudolph, Carol. *Spider Woman*. Santa Fe: Ancient City Press, 1997.

RECOMMENDED LINKS

Edgar Cayce's Website:
http://www.edgarcayce.org
I was introduced to Edgar Cayce over 25 years ago by my dear friend Patrick. He simply gave me a book about him, called *There is a River*. Little did I know that this man's life would incorporate into my life in so many ways. No further words needed, other than to encourage you to immerse yourself in the A.R.E. website and explore!

To subscribe to Edgar Cayce's Thought for the Day Emails:
http://www.edgarcayce.org/quoteofday.asp
Excellent daily reminders to help you contemplate your own thoughts, emotions, and life, and to help you move toward a more unified Being.

Julian Treasure's TED Talk on Sound:
http://www.ted.com/talks/julian_treasure_the_4_ways_sound_affects_us/transcript
The importance of sound was revealed to me, including the crucial function sound has in establishing peace in our internal world and in the world at large. Julian's TED Talk is a good place to start to understand the significance of sound and the role it can play in an individual's health and balance, along with healing the world.

FURTHER READING

Animal Speak: The Spiritual & Magical Powers of Creatures Great & Small, by Ted Andrews – Ted was a very knowledgeable man regarding the animal kingdom. His insights into the animal archetypes are unparalleled. This book and the one below assisted me in understanding the multitude of animal communications and symbols that were coming through to me during my initiation as a Medicine Woman. To this day, the animal realm assists me enormously in my Medicine Woman work.

Animal-Wise: The Spirit Language and Signs of Nature, by Ted Andrews – See above. Expands the repertoire of animals started in the above book.

The Four Agreements, by Don Miguel Ruiz – Excellent beginner's book for acquainting yourself with yourself. Start with "being impeccable with your word" – that is, being honest, and revealing the range of sealed-off thoughts and emotions to your conscious self.

The Healer's Manual: A Beginner's Guide to Vibrational Therapies, by Ted Andrews – Excellent book to understand our different bodies, the concept of vibration, and to start to tap into the "healer within."

How to Be Compassionate, by His Holiness the Dalai Lama – Fabulous teachings for what to do and how to work the moment when pulled off-balance, when we do not see peace, compassion, or perfection.

How to Be Your Dog's Best Friend: The Classic Training Manual for Dog Owners, by The Monks of New Skete – Great tips to apply in the journey and dance of life with your dog; and furthermore, it has much depth to be uncovered in the spiritual and metaphysical arenas.

Kundalini and the Chakras: A Practical Manual, by Genevieve Lewis Paulson – One of the best books I have found that explains Kundalini energy in a very detailed, clear, and, based on my experience, very accurate and current manner. A must for practically everyone.

The Language of Letting Go: Daily Meditations for Codependents, by Melody Beattie – The idea is to read this book relative to the co-dependency within us, i.e. our co-dependency with our emotions, thoughts, and other aspects of our separate Selves.

The Law of One: The Ra Material, Books I-IV, by Elkins, Rueckert, and McCarty – For advanced students. Personally, this book has assisted me continuously on many levels. It helps with understanding the enormous existence of life beyond our earth. This is similar to explaining to a seven-year-old the depth, complexity, and immensity of the world beyond the three blocks of the house that the child is familiar with.

Love, Medicine & Miracles, by Bernie S. Siegel, M.D. – Superb book for those who have experienced or are experiencing cancer and/or various medical issues. Assists with tapping into the "healer within."

The Mystical Magical Marvelous World of Dreams, by Wilda B. Tanner – One of my favorite books of dreams. Very accurate, thorough, detailed, and overall wonderful.

On Death and Dying, Elizabeth Kübler-Ross, M.D. – World-known author that talks about the stages of grief during the process of death, both for the dying and the ones left behind. If you are experiencing, or know someone who is experiencing, death, it would be a very welcoming book.

Sacred Contracts: Awakening Your Divine Potential, by Caroline Myss – For those who are serious about working on and getting to know themselves, this is an excellent book. It deals with the archetypes that we embody. Learning to be conscious of these blueprints that we personify is an important goal, as is learning to work with them.

Zen in the Martial Arts, by Joe Hyams – Fabulous, concise material. Joe Hyams studied with Bruce Lee and writes very effectively to communicate spiritual teachings learned in the dojo and how he applied them to daily life. One of my favorites.

Please visit Lizette's website
www.MedicineWomanSpeaks.com
for updated links and recommended readings.

Ceremonial Healing Sessions

Medicine Woman Lizette
is available remotely for:

Life/Death Transition Sessions

For individuals who are near death, in a coma, or in hospice. The purpose is to prepare the physical, emotional, and mental bodies for optimum vibration to facilitate an easier Life/Death transition. The higher the mental and emotional vibration of the person experiencing death, the easier the letting go and the more welcoming the birth into the next world.

Aura Clearing Sessions

WITH EMPHASIS ON THOSE EXPERIENCING CANCER

Clearing and balancing of emotional, mental, and/or physical energy. By nature, we collect debris in our auras. A clearing helps to remove debris and clear energy blockages, and to provide overall energy balance and alignment. Excellent for anyone and everyone.

**THESE TWO SESSIONS ARE ALSO
AVAILABLE FOR PETS**

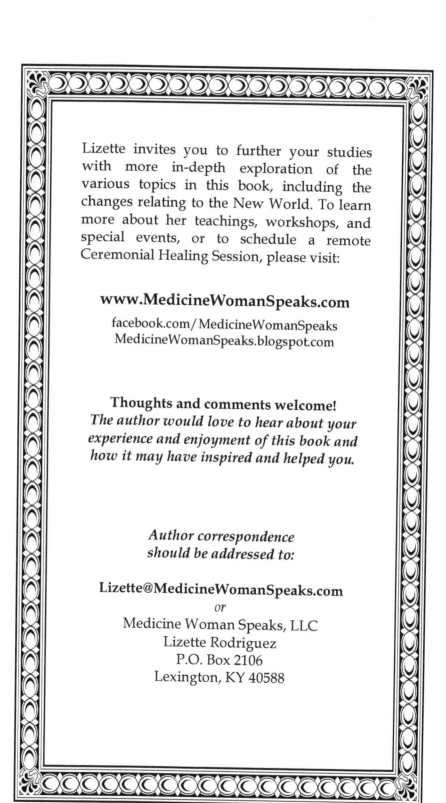

Lizette invites you to further your studies with more in-depth exploration of the various topics in this book, including the changes relating to the New World. To learn more about her teachings, workshops, and special events, or to schedule a remote Ceremonial Healing Session, please visit:

www.MedicineWomanSpeaks.com

facebook.com/MedicineWomanSpeaks
MedicineWomanSpeaks.blogspot.com

Thoughts and comments welcome!
The author would love to hear about your experience and enjoyment of this book and how it may have inspired and helped you.

*Author correspondence
should be addressed to:*

Lizette@MedicineWomanSpeaks.com
or
Medicine Woman Speaks, LLC
Lizette Rodriguez
P.O. Box 2106
Lexington, KY 40588

Coming Soon!

Greeting Cards

Various quotes from this book will be available as Greeting Cards.

Book

Keep an eye out for Lizette's forthcoming book, *Beyond the Zodiac Signs*. This is a translation of a book by the same name in Spanish by Dr. Arturo Estrada, Lizette's metaphysic, esoteric and spiritual teacher. Intended for the advanced and dedicated student, this book will present esoteric and metaphysical exercises to balance and realign negative astrological characteristics. It is now time for the world to learn these extraordinary teachings that have opened up to humanity. The Spanish title, *Más Allá de los Signos*, will also be available.

Petite Inspirational Box

Various business card-sized inspirational quotes ready to be passed along to family, friends, coworkers, or anyone you want to uplift and inspire. Stored in its own decorative box.

© 2007 Sandra Castro SYC Media

My wish is that the eternal flame within you
light with joy every word, thought,
and action that you take.

- Medicine Woman Lizette

About the Author

Lizette has been studying for twenty years with Dr. Arturo Estrada, a medical and metaphysical doctor and a living Bodhisattva of the Venerable Master Hermes Tyr Iadou. Dr. Estrada's practice is located in Bogota, Colombia, her home country. She works alongside the Logos, acting as a springboard and catalyst for our current evolution, an exciting and great task at these times. A new light configuration has emerged and is manifesting its complete radiance and structure. Lizette's goal is to encourage and support an increase of awareness between the manifesting light configuration and the opportunities for health, growth, and balance.

She has been psychic and intuitive all her life and studied palmistry, astrology, martial arts, as well as the works of Kentucky native, Edgar Cayce. During this lifetime, she has had a gravitational pull towards the esoteric and metaphysical, along with an intense curiosity, wonder, and love for nature, and animals. From a very young age, she has wanted to heal with her hands.

Her incredible mystical journey began when she suffered an injury to her etheric body, causing intense physical nerve pain throughout her entire physical body – particularly through the arms, hands, and neck. She experienced the pain continuously 24/7 for about six months. The struggles that ensued and the emotional and mental dips into the depths of despair and turmoil on all fronts – emotional, mental, physical, and spiritual – led her to rise and pierce through to her Higher Self and emerge to new heights. Part of this mystical experience included her walk through the Dark Night of the Soul and her initiation into the world of the Medicine Woman.

Lizette lives in Lexington, Kentucky with her daughter and three cats. This is her first book.

Lightning Source UK Ltd.
Milton Keynes UK
UKHW01f1809010818
326639UK00001B/101/P